26

Catalog
of Chess
Mistakes

PRINO U 86

Other books by the author
published by
the David McKay Company:

THE BEST GAMES OF BORIS SPASSKY

THE ART OF DEFENSE IN CHESS

PAWN STRUCTURE CHESS

Catalog
of Chess
Mistakes

by
Andrew Soltis
International Chess Master

DAVID McKAY COMPANY, INC.
NEW YORK

Library of Congress Cataloging in Publication Data

Soltis, Andrew.
  Catalog of chess mistakes.

  1. Chess. I. Title.
GV1449.5.S64   794.1'2   79-11090
ISBN 0-679-13250-3

7 8 9 10

MANUFACTURED IN THE UNITED STATES OF AMERICA

Contents

Catalog
of Chess
Mistakes

The Game of Mistakes

Chess is a game of bad moves. It is, in fact, the game that most depends on error. No game has a greater variety of ways of going wrong or gives you as many opportunities—dozens on every move. Other games depend heavily on chance or on the mastery of some relatively limited skills. But a chess game is decided by the failings of one of the players.

Yet we refuse to recognize this. We like to think the game is a battle between good moves and better moves. When we win, we tell ourselves—and anyone who will listen—that the critical difference was our fine maneuvering, our positional cunning, or our tactical ingenuity. When we lose, well, it was a stupid mistake—as if errors were an aberration, an extraordinary accident. Mistakes can only be messy, ugly, and disruptive, we say.

Regardless of our own success, we like to think a chess game should be won, not lost. (We thereby ignore that most vital skill, the ability to exploit enemy mistakes.) We try to elevate the game to some level it can never achieve—at least not while it's being played by humans.

The masters know better. They know that a well-played game is not an error-free game. There are errors of varying magnitudes, and each game is sure to hold some small mistakes. "Chess is the struggle against error," said Johannes Zukertort, one of the greatest players of the last century. Victory belongs to the player who struggles best—not just against an opponent, but against himself.

And the fact is that most games, even at the grandmaster level,

1

are constant struggles. Look at the 1972 world championship match, the most talked-about chess contest ever. What were the memorable moves when Fischer met Spassky?

The ones that stand out include: Fischer's strange loss of a piece in the first game; Spassky's double-barreled oversight in the eighth game, losing the Exchange on the 15th move and a pawn on the 19th move; the Russian's sloppy opening and long defense in the 13th game, which ended with suicidal collapse on the 69th move; Spassky's careless oversight in the following game. Suffice it to say that the match ended with a mistake, Spassky's erroneous sealed move in the final game. Mistakes *were* the match.

Unique? Hardly. There were more good moves than bad ones in the 1972 match, but the bad ones counted more. The same can be said of the 1978 world championship match and most other contests that come to mind.

What Is a Mistake?

"Where did I make my mistake?" asked the loser, an Australian master. "I didn't know what to say," said the winner, a Russian grandmaster. There wasn't one move you could pin the blame on. Yet by the 14th move White was already in grave trouble.

Hanks–Kotov, Melbourne 1963—*1. P–Q4 P–Q3 2. P–K4 P–KN3 3. N–QB3 B–N2 4. B–K2 N–QB3 5. B–K3 N–B3 6. P–Q5 N–QN1 7. N–B3 P–B4 8. P–KR3 0–0 9. N–Q2 N–K1 10. 0–0 N–B2 11. P–QR4 QN–R3 12. P–B4 N–N5 13. N–B4 P–B4! 14. P–K5 P–N3! 15. B–B3 B–QR3 16. P–QN3 BxN 17. PxB PxP 18. PxP BxP 19. R–R3 N–K1! 20. P–Q6 NxP! 21. BxR QxB 22. Q–K2 BxN 23. RxB N–K5 24. B–Q2 P–K4! 25. B–R6 NxR 26. QxP N–K7ch 27. K–B2 R–B2 28. QxN Q–K5 and Black won.*

Position after 14. . . . P–N3

White didn't have to throw himself on a sword with 25. B–R6?!, but he would have been quite lost after 25. R–QN3 NxP and 26. . . . N–Q5. The search for a "losing move" must begin earlier.

White lost because of several almost miniscule failings. He compromised his center early (6. P–Q5?!) and then lost time (8. P–KR3? rather than 8. N–Q2!). He had to make further concessions (11. P–QR4?!—to avoid . . . P–QN4 when he plays N–B4) and then gave away the last hope of supporting his center (12. P–B4?). By the 15th move he saw he was losing his QP or KP, and everything followed from that.

None of these moves seems fatal. Yet added up, they destroyed White before the second cup of coffee. Nor was Black free from error. With 7. . . . P–B3! he could have begun the attack on the White center even earlier.

We can recognize the truly bad moves when they are punished quickly. It is the other 98 percent of a chess game that leaves us confused.

A typical move has good and bad qualities. On the simplest level, a move—any move—attacks and protects certain squares while withdrawing contact from others. A move may strengthen our pawn structure, expand the scope of our bishops, and make a major threat, all at once. But whether the move is good or bad depends on an evaluation of its minuses as well as its pluses. That same move may walk into a tactical pin. It may remove a piece from a theater subject to imminent attack. It may reduce tension when you want to heighten it. Or its biggest fault may simply be that there is a superior move available.

Spassky–Fischer, Match 1972
Black to move

A mistake is a mistake on its demerits, not on its merits—or press notices. In this critical point in the 1972 match, Spassky, on the verge of regaining the momentum after his costly blunders, looks for counterplay in a poor ending. The position appears quiet, but White threatens to sidetrack Black with R–KB4 and R–R4–R7ch.

1. . . .   **R–R1**

"Obvious and strong," said Reuben Fine. "A fine reply," said C. H. O'D. Alexander. "If BxR RxB Black has all the play," said Svetozar Gligoric, and Samuel Reshevsky agreed. So did many others.

But Fischer's close supporters in Iceland cursed 1. . . . R–R1? The rook move, though spectacular in appearance, only confused Black's pieces after 2. B–B6! With the correct 1. . . . R–KN1! Black could have transferred his pieces to their prime real estate —the king to the queenside with . . . K–K1 and later . . . K–Q2–B3, and the rooks to the kingside with . . . R–R2 and . . . R–KB2.

The move played was an error, although its punishment was disguised (the game became much longer as a result and should have been drawn) and although some of the world's best players praised it. The good points of 1. . . . R–R1, such as stopping R–KB4–R4, were smothered by its bad points.

Even when we know a mistake has been made—because punishment is swift in coming—we may not know what exactly went wrong.

Levenfish–Flamberg, Vilna 1912—*1. P–K4 P–K4 2. N–KB3 N–QB3 3. B–N5 P–QR3 4. B–R4 N–B3 5. Q–K2 P–QN4 6. B–N3 B–B4 7. P–QR4 R–QN1 8. PxP PxP 9. N–B3 0–0 10. P–Q3 P–Q3 11. B–N5*

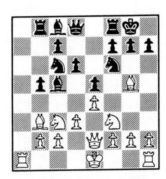

Position after 11. B–N5

In a position of rapidly sharpening play, Black continued:

11. . . .	B–KN5
12. N–Q5	N–Q5
13. NxN!	BxQ
14. BxN!	R–R1
15. KxB	Q–N1
16. N–B6	

White's minor pieces begin to swarm over the board, and after 16. . . . Q–N2 17. N(5)–K7ch K–R1 18. B–N5 RxR 19. RxR P–B3 20. B–K3 BxB 21. PxB P–N3 22. B–Q5 Q–N3 23. P–QN4 P–B4 24. P–N3 P–B5 25. NPxP PxP 26. P–Q4! PxP 27. KxP K–N2 28. B–K6! Black could save his queen from the threat of B–Q7 (followed by N–Q5 and R–R7) only by giving up more material. White eventually won.

It's safe to say that Black lost the game early on, around moves 11 to 13. We may be able to pick out a single losing move. But there are so many reasons for error and so many ways to err that we can only guess at the nature of the decisive mistake.

For example, we might say Black lost because of a faulty attitude. He could have equalized chances with the safe 11. . . . B–K3 but sought the advantage instead: *he tried for too much*. Or he may have been *overconfident* because of his faith in book knowledge. Only a few months before this game was played, another game (Alapin–Leonhardt, Pistyan 1912) followed the same moves but Black obtained the advantage—13. BxN? R–R1! 14. Q–Q1 (or 14. BxQ RxRch 15. K–Q2 RxR with material loss) 14. . . . RxR 15. QxR NxB! 16. PxN PxB 17. P–N4 P–B3.

Or we could blame Black's downfall on an *oversight*, a failure to consider the queen sacrifice (13. NxN!). The term "oversight" tends to be misleading. Nobody guesses every move his opponent makes. At the master level players "overlook" their opponent's middlegame moves as much as 50 percent of the time. But most of the time the failure to anticipate a move isn't punished. Black of course knew that 13. NxN was possible. His "oversight"—if it was one—consisted of not evaluating the sacrifice sufficiently. What he overlooked was not the move but its strength.

Perhaps Black did examine the sacrifice but *miscalculated*. He could have erred by overlooking White's *order of moves*. (For example, he may have counted on 14. N–B6 and satisfied himself that Black was okay after 14. . . . R–R1! 15. KxB Q–Q2.)

Or he may have *assumed* incorrectly. (He may have played 12. . . . N–Q5 thinking that after the queen sacrifice he could meet 14. BxN with 14. . . . Q–Q2 15. NxB P–B3 16. N–K7ch K–R1 17. B–KR4 P–N4! 18. BxNP P–B3. But after 14. BxN he may have suddenly realized that 14. . . . Q–Q2 could be met by 15. N–B5!; e.g., 15. . . . B–R4 16. QN–K7ch K–R1 17. BxP mate or 15. . . . . KR–K1 16. KxB).

Or Black may have gone wrong in his calculations by missing White's *quiet move*, 15. KxB. That recapture doesn't seem aggressive enough until you see that 15. . . . RxR 16. RxR PxB 17. N–B6 traps Black's queen (17. . . . Q–Q2 18. NxPch). Black may have underestimated a move, 15. KxB, that doesn't attack anything and defends very little—yet it wins.

Finally, we could say the real error came earlier, at move 11, when Black rushed into playing an apparently good move when there was an even *better move*. His error had less to do with tactics or calculation than with the practical process of choosing a move. (With 11. . . . P–R3 Black forces a favorable exchange on his KB3 since 12. B–R4 takes the sting out of White's attack; e.g., 12. . . . B–KN5! 13. N–Q5 P–N4!.)

Any one of these errors—or a combination of them—may have been the culprit. Only the loser knew for sure.

Bronstein–Botvinnik, Match 1951
White to move

The next position highlights one of the most spectacular blunders in chess history. David Bronstein was leading in a match for the world title when he threw away a certain draw in this game. He eventually drew the match—letting the champion retain the title—and never got close to the championship again.

Everyone, it seems, who played over the game knew for certain why Bronstein played *1. K–B2??*, the losing move. Obviously he had calculated the variation 1. . . . K–B6 2. N–K6 P–K7 3. N–Q4ch followed by 4. NxP (with a draw) but overlooked *1. . . . K–N6!* which wins for Black (2. K–Q1 K–B7 3. N–K6 P–K7ch; 2. N–K6 P–K7 3. K–Q2 K–B7).

Everyone knew. But only Bronstein knew for certain. Twenty-five years later he explained for the first time what went wrong. He had seen 1. N–K6ch, the drawing move, and 2. N–Q4. But he had been playing for a win since the middlegame, and with the game's end in sight, he relaxed: "Now that time pressure was over and it was necessary only to give check N–K6, I began to recall . . . the opening of the game, smiling at the refinement of his eighth move for a whole 45 minutes, and then unexpectedly I took hold of the king. It had to move . . ."

So the world championship may have been lost through day-dreaming and a slip of the finger—not the miscalculation the chess world assumed.

The Other Side: Helping Him Err

To play superior chess you need a realistic attitude toward error. This involves something of a paradox: you should play as if your opponent will make error-free moves. But you should give him the opportunity to make errors.

There is a distinct temptation to make trappy moves, that is, moves that are of questionable value but which set traps for the enemy. This is a bad habit to get into, no matter how often it succeeds. If you expect to improve in chess, you'll eventually reach the level of skill where trappy moves are recognized instantly for what they are.

But there is another lesson for the improving player to learn. Too many inexperienced players try to overwhelm the enemy. They never miss an opportunity to make a threat or press an attack. And when they face equally inexperienced opponents, more often than not the threats and attacks will be poorly handled. But when they meet more experienced players they find that forcing the tempo of play actually eases the task of defense by their opponents.

Why? *Because players usually err when faced with a choice of reasonable alternatives.* If there is very little choice—if your opponent can choose between meeting your threat or getting mated in one move—there isn't much room for mistake.

Anatoly Karpov, the current world champion, never fails to give his opponents enough rope for their own hanging. He rarely forces the action from an early point in the game on. Instead, he prefers to overwhelm his foes with choices, knowing that only the very best players will pass the test.

Position after 13. . . . B–N2

Torre–Karpov, Bad Lauterberg 1977—*1. P–K4 P–QB4 2. N–KB3 P–K3 3. P–Q4 PxP 4. NxP P–QR3 5. P–QB4 Q–B2 6. P–QR3 N–KB3 7. N–QB3 N–B3 8. B–K3 B–K2 9. R–B1 N–K4!? 10. B–K2 N–N3 11. 0–0 P–N3 12. P–B4 0–0 13. P–QN4 B–N2*

Note Black's opening play. He lets White put pieces pretty much wherever he likes and makes little effort to find immediate counterplay. Instead, Black maneuvers his pieces, especially his QN, to take the sting out of White's *natural* moves of aggression.

In many comparable positions White obtains a strong game with P–K5 or P–KB5, followed by attack in the center or kingside. Here, however, Black has made sure that any such advance would be an error. After P–KB5 Black drops his knight on K4 and puts White's QBP and KP under enough pressure to defuse any initiative. After 14. P–K5 N–K1 White's center is overextended and ready to be dissolved by . . . P–Q3, and then Black is at least equal.

Karpov hasn't actually prevented P–K5 or P–KB5. In fact, he seems to be provoking those moves. He is giving White the opportunity to go wrong with these pawn advances.

| 14. B–Q3 | QR–B1 |
| 15. N–N3 | P–Q3 |

White had been threatening 16. P–QB5, which would now lead to another attractive but faulty liquidation in the center. White recognizes that there will be no dramatic changes in the center and that he must therefore find a plan on the wings.

His choice remains enormous. He can try the kingside with R–B3 followed by attacking KR7 with R–R3, P–KN4–5, and Q–R5. Black should be able to handle that idea comfortably with . . . KR–K1 and . . . N–B1. However, White might be able to shift his attack from KR7 to other points on the kingside with a subsequent P–KB5.

Or White could attack on the queenside by aiming at the Black pawns and preparing P–QB5 or P–QR4–5. This is a properly safe plan, and White's next several moves advance it.

16. Q–K2	KR–K1
17. P–R3	N–Q2
18. Q–KB2	B–R1
19. R–B2	Q–N1
20. KR–B1	

Black's moves seem clumsy and ineffective. Yet he has skillfully anticipated the attack on his QNP and the P–QB5 break (21. P–QB5 NPxP 22. BxRP R–B2 only favors Black after 23. PxP QxN or 23. N–N5 R–B3). He can sit and wait for something to happen, knowing that his position is secure. Or he can give White some more rope.

20. . . .   B–R5!

This can't be any worse than the immediate 20. . . . B–Q1 or 20. . . . B–KB3, the moves Black might have been expected to play. But with 20. . . . B–R5 Black also gives White a chance to weaken his kingside.

21. P–N3?

Often a move so weakening as to be rejected under normal circumstances is chosen when you can play it without loss of time. Here P–KN3 is a free move for White, so to speak, since it attacks Black bishop. But it is still a poor move, for it weakens the kingside and the long diagonal (QR8–KR1).

21. . . .	B–Q1
22. N–Q2	B–KB3
23. P–KR4?!	

By giving White more rope, Black provokes a kingside attack that should fail. White's plan is consistent with his 21st move, which he still believes to be good. This illustrates another point about error: you are much more sensitive to the possibility of making a mistake when you have a bad game; but when you are optimistic about your position, your early warning system tends to close down.

Notice that Black was threatening absolutely nothing.

23. . . .	P–R3
24. P–R5	N(3)–B1
25. P–N4?!	N–R2!

Position after 25. . . . N–R2

So far White has made some minor strategic mistakes and has earned a dangerous-looking but risky position. Black's last move prepares a powerful stroke in the center, . . . P–K4!. Without White's kingside demonstration, . . . P–K4 would be a major positional concession, giving away the KB4 and Q4 squares to White and making N–Q5! a winning idea. But under the new circumstances, Black will be able to develop a grip on the black kingside squares if he plays 26. . . . P–K4; e.g., 27. P–KB5 B–N4! 28. N–B3 BxB 29. QxB N(Q)–B3 30. N–KR2 N–N4 or 27. Q–N3 PxP 28. BxBP N–K4 29. N–Q5 BxN 30. KPxB N–N4 (or 30. BPxB RxR 31. RxR P–QN4 followed by . . . N–N4 or . . . B–N4).

But what else can White do? With 26. N–B3 he stops 26. . . . P–K4 but allows 26. . . . BxN 27. RxB N(Q)–B3 winning a pawn. He certainly doesn't like that, but he doesn't want to go on the defensive after . . . P–K4. Faced with yet another choice, this time between pessimistic alternatives, White makes another error: he goes for broke.

26. P–K5?!	PxP
27. P–KN5	

Now with 27. . . . RPxP 28. BxNch! KxB 29. PxNP White has a winning game (29. . . . B–K2 30. QxP). But his panic after 25. . . . N–R2 has provoked a miscalculation.

27. . . .	KPxP!

White's choices from here on are either bad or worse. Recapturing on KB4 is bad, but 28. PxB PxB 29. QxP QNxP (with a deadly kingside attack coming up for Black) is worse.

28. BxBP	B–K4
29. P–N6?!	PxP
30. PxP	BxB
31. PxNch	K–R1
32. R–B1	R–B1
33. B–K4	N–K4!

Now Black's threat of 34. . . . N–N5 or 34. . . . NxP ends the contest quickly. White played *34. Q–N2*, and after *34. . . . NxP* he resigned.

Taking Stock

Experience, as defined by Oscar Wilde, is what we call the record of our past mistakes. Recognizing the inevitability of mistakes is a good first step to dealing with them. The next step is understanding what kind of mistakes we make. Only after that can we take action to eliminate them.

You can begin by collecting as many of your past game scores as you can find. (If you don't record your games, start now.) Try to locate a large number. Most people keep only their wins, not realizing that you learn much more from your losses.

Ideally, you should have a balanced assortment of at least forty games—some wins, more losses; some games with the White pieces, some with Black. It doesn't matter whether the games are played in club tournaments or on park benches. As long as you were trying to find the best moves, you'll have a solid documentary record to work with.

Examine each game with the scrutiny of your severest critic. Even if you won a game there are sure to be some blind spots—second-best moves, sloppy thinking—to be found among your moves. Try to remember what your thoughts were as you played each move. Did you consider several alternatives or just play the first good-looking idea? Did you think you were winning all along, or were you just trying to hang on?

This won't require as much work as it may seem. In an average game of forty moves, the first seven or so moves are part of your opening arsenal. (Maybe more.) You don't really think about and evaluate these moves the way you would move 23. There are also bound to be several automatic captures and recaptures, as well as forced responses to enemy threats. You may find that only twenty to twenty-five moves of the forty required real choice.

Play over each game a few times. This will take a lot of effort but is well worth a few lost Sunday afternoons. Question any move that looks suspicious—even if it wasn't punished. Then compare the questionable moves with this checklist.

(1) What kind of error is it? Positional? Tactical? Strategic? Poor Attitude? Each of the following chapters will discuss a different kind of error.

(2) How serious would the error be if punished? Is it a minor error or a game-losing blunder?

(3) When was the error made? Opening? Middlegame? Endgame?

(4) What was the status of the game when you committed the error? Did you think you were winning easily? Slightly superior? Even? Dead lost?

(5) How were your errors spaced? Did you make two or three bad moves in a row? One every ten moves?

Remember that there may be several reasons that a move is bad. Each can be considered a separate error for the purposes of this self-analysis. If possible, you should keep a record of how much time you spent on each move. This helps in understanding how a mistake came about. For example, if you blunder away a rook after thinking only ten seconds, you may place the blame on the poor attitude of carelessness or overconfidence. But if you thought twenty minutes on the losing move, you will have to look elsewhere.

By examining the responses to this checklist you can develop a fairly accurate Error Profile of yourself. You'll know whether you are prone to blunder or lose more often through an accumulation of minor errors. You may learn, further, that you are most liable to blunder in the ending than the middlegame, or that you make more of your serious errors in unfavorable positions (Despair or Pessimism?) than in favorable ones. You'll know when to be on guard against your natural tendencies to err (Just as your position is improving? Just after a previous error?). You may find that you made more errors in games you eventually won than in games you lost.

Once you've developed this Error Profile you'll know, in short, what part of your game you need to work on away from the tournament hall and what to watch out for when you are at the board. Self-awareness is the name of the game.

"How Can I Lose?"

When you're at the board, you look for good moves—either good moves for you to play or dangerous to you if he plays them. It may seem like toying with fire, but you should also be looking for bad moves. A good sense of danger, of knowing how you can go wrong in a particular position, can help enormously.

Garcia–Ivkov, Havana 1965
Black to move

Black has so great a material advantage he doesn't have to worry about losing a pawn or two. But he can't stop worrying, period. In fact, this is the perfect time to wonder about losing. Perhaps, there is nothing you can do that will lose the game quickly. But it doesn't hurt to look. Black didn't.

1. . . .	**P–Q6??**
2. B–B3	**Resigns**

Black lost simply because he did not look for a losing error. He probably didn't think losing was possible. You might say that he made an oversight, perhaps thinking that he could count on his knight to stop 3. Q–N7 mate (forgetting about 3. Q–R8 mate). This may have been the case. But the root cause of this oversight was carelessness bred by a poor attitude. Black didn't look for an error.

By asking yourself "How can I lose?" you can anticipate many tactical surprises. If you play serious chess with a clock, you can use the time while your opponent is thinking to search for possible traps.

This safeguard is useful in a number of situations, not just when there is a specific tactical danger you should know about. Take the following, an apparently innocent endgame from a Soviet women's championship.

Kakhabrishvilli–Zaitseva, Tiflis 1976
White to move

Black is the only player with serious winning chances, but victory depends on White's cooperation. Even if White were to lose both of her pawns, she could still draw by keeping her king at KR1. Then Black could never drive the king out of the corner or promote her own pawn. A draw would be inevitable.

Yet White managed to lose. She lost, in fact, because she looked only for a way of drawing the position. By doing so, she completely overlooked a losing method.

| 1. K–R4 | B–B3ch |
| 2. K–R5 | |

White is in a hurry to force a draw by liquidating the board's last pawns. She want to play P–KR4 and P–N5, disdaining the sure draw to be had by keeping her king around KR1. What she's overlooked is cute. But she would have seen it had she asked, "How can I lose?"

| 2. ... | B–N4! |
| 3. P–R4 | K–B5!! |

It's too late to ask. After 4. PxB PxP White has obtained material equality but will lose the king-and-pawn endgame. Even if she refuses to take the bishop, her king is too far away from KR1 to stop Black's KRP (4. K–N6 KxP 5. P–R5 B–K6 6. K–B6 KxP and ... K–N5).

"The mistakes are there," Savielly Tartakower said, "waiting to be made."

Tactical Errors

Separating tactical errors from the other ways of losing a chess game seems, at first, an impossible task. When you first learn to play the game *all* your major errors are tactical.

You lose because you permit a knight to fork your king and queen, or you overlook a mate in one. After a while, you learn to avoid these pitfalls, but your mistakes remain essentially tactical. You walk into a pin or some kind of double attack by enemy pieces and eventually have to surrender material. You have to learn a good deal about the game before you even get the opportunity (!) to lose through positional or strategic errors.

After you've matured as a player and have learned the breadth of possible chess mistakes, the distinction between tactical and nontactical errors becomes blurred. This is because almost all games, even at the highest of grandmaster ranks, are ultimately decided by tactical means. A player may weaken his pawn structure—a positional error—at move 15, or he may choose a bad plan—a strategic error—at move 20. But when he is finally punished for his sins—on move 40 or 60 or even 90—it will be done tactically. Eventually his position will deteriorate to the point that enemy pieces penetrate and create the knight forks, mating threats, and double attacks that can no longer be resisted.

What separates purely tactical errors from the others is the immediacy of punishment and the carelessness that leads to their commission. When you permit a knight fork you are penalized right then and there with a loss of material. The cause of your error is easy to understand: you overlooked the tactical trick that exploited the error. When you lose you know very well why and how you lost.

Allowing Mate

Of all the punishing strokes to overlook, the worst is mate. You can lose a pawn or a piece and still continue the fight—perhaps even win—depending on your opponent's ability to play without serious error. But when you walk into a mate, it's time to set the pieces up for the next game.

Masic–Mariotti, Sombor 1969
White to move

How can a good player overlook a mate? For the same reason that he can permit a fork or a pin—or ruin his pawn structure or lose a winning endgame: there is so much to look for in a chess game that you can only focus on a limited number of considerations. In many cases a master will make a bad error, which loses the game immediately, because he is trying to avoid the many minor mistakes that might cost him the game in the long run.

In the diagram Black is intent on breaking through on the queenside where his strength is massed. After 1. PxP PxP Black will be able to pile up on the vulnerable White QRP after 2. . . . P–N5 and 3. . . . N–N2. If White does nothing about the queenside, Black will penetrate with 1. . . . PxP; e.g., 2. PxP R–N7 3. R–B2 R(1)–QN1, or 2. NxP NxN 3. BxN N–N3 4. B–K2 P–R4 and 5. . . . P–R5.

These considerations explain why after

1. R–B3

Black innocently played . . .

1. . . .   **PxP??**

And had to resign after

2. N–B5ch!

White will continue 2. . . . PxN 3. R–KN1 and mate with 4. R–R3. There is no defense. Black lost because mate was the last thing in the world to look for. He thought.

This, then, is the cardinal rule of chess. Don't forget about checkmate. The position on the board may be a quiet middle-game or routine endgame. There are certain to be a great many things to look for in the position. But don't forget the error that hurts the most.

It can happen before you've settled in your seat:

Position after 11. . . . P–QN3

This position derives from a relatively innocuous opening—
1. P–K4 P–QB3 2. P–Q4 P–Q4 3. N–QB3 PxP 4. NxP N–Q2 5. B–QB4 KN–B3 6. N–N5 P–K3 7. Q–K2 N–N3 8. B–Q3 P–KR3 9. N(5)–B3 P–B4 10. PxP QN–Q2 11. P–QN4 P–QN3!

White has won a pawn but cannot keep it (12. PxP BxPch and . . . QxP). In fact, White seems to have seriously weakened his position with 11. P–QN4, creating weaknesses all over his queen-side.

12. N–Q4!?

This tricky move seems pointless. After 12. . . . PxP Black's advantage appears obvious after 13. PxP BxP or 13. N–B6 Q–B2. Seeing this, Black might continue with

12. . . .	PxP??
13. N–B6	Q–B2

But he will be suddenly reminded that all the positional advantages in the world won't make up for . . .

14. QxPch!	PxQ
15. B–N6 mate.	

Removal of Defender

When I was just beginning to learn the game, one thing always struck me about the moves of more experienced players. During the early stages of a game most of the pieces, White and Black, were protected by friendly pieces.

This seemed astonishing at the time. In my early games it was impossible to keep half my pieces safe from capture at any given moment. I didn't deliberately put my men on squares subject to enemy attack. But inevitably they were captured through the usual assortment of tactical ideas: skewers and forks and pins. The only time my material was completely safe was when the pieces were suffocating along the first and second ranks.

More experienced players know how to advance *and* keep their pieces in mutual protection. It becomes so natural that Mikhail Botvinnik surprised his colleagues when he praised his rival, Tigran Petrosian, after losing the world championship to him. Botvinnik could have cited the new champion's positional depth or endgame mastery or calculating ability. But what Botvinnik cited above all was simpler: "Notice how his pieces are always protected."

In its basic form, this is a game of weaknesses. Each player has a set of weaknesses to defend—his king, perhaps, as well as some pawns, key squares, and pieces—and some targets of the same nature to attack. Eventually there is a tactical breakthrough because of an imbalance of attack and protection: there are more pieces attacking a weakness than defending it.

The tactical device most often used to accomplish this imbalance is the Removal of the Defender. Take this position.

Keres–Averbakh, Zurich 1953
White to move

White's pawns at Q4 and QB4 are his chief weaknesses. The QBP is defended twice and attacked once—a balance of protection. The White defenders cannot be pushed back, exchanged off, or lured away. But the QP is attacked twice and defended only once.

There are five ways to defend the QP. White can bring his knight to KB3. But that defender can be removed by 1. N–B3 BxN. White can also play 1. QR–Q1, but the QBP could later become a target. And since White doesn't like to deprive his knight of its pawn anchor, he rejects 1. P–Q5. That leaves the KR as the defender, and it can take up its responsibility on Q1 or KB4. The ambitious White grandmaster wanted to keep the possible play along the KB-file, so he played:

1. R–B4??

Black replied:

1. ...   **P–KN4!**

And an embarrassed White saw that he must retreat his defender and lose the pawn that solidifies his game. Black's progress toward victory was rapid *(2. R–KB2 QxQP 3. QxQ RxQ 4.*

QR–KB1 R–Q3 5. P–KR4 PxP 6. R–B4 R–B4 7. N–N4 NxN 8. RxNch K–B1 9. BxP B–R3 10. R[1]–B4 R–R3), and he eventually won.

The number of variations on this theme is considerable, but the key element is easy to recognize. A defending piece is taken out of commission by some means—a threat of capture, or an equal exchange of piece for piece, or a threat elsewhere which requires the services of the defender.

This much can be understood by anyone who learns the moves of the pieces. What makes the tactical struggles difficult is the variety and complexity of several simultaneous battles—each one made up of attacking and defending pieces.

Georgieva–Konarkovska-Sokolov, Belgrade 1977
Black to move

Black has sacrificed a rook for two pawns and a strong attack, whose current focal point is KR7 and other squares around the White king. White must protect his KR2 from a possible . . . Q–R7 mate. With this in mind, Black can play 1. . . . R–K6!. If White responds 2. Q–QB2, threatening a strong check of his own at QB8, Black has a choice among a promising ending with 2. . . . QxBch, a continuation of the attack with 2. . . . R–R6ch, or even a perpetual attack on the White Queen (2. . . . R–QB6 3. Q–K2 R–K6 4. Q–KN2 R–KN6). White can never play QxR because of . . . Q–R7 mate.

1. . . .	R–R6ch?
2. K–N1	B–B4ch?

Black could have used the Removal of Defender device to win back the rook immediately with 2. . . . Q–N6ch 3. Q–N2 B–B4ch 4. R–B2 BxRch or 3. B–N2 R–R8ch! 4. KxR Q–R7 mate.

3. R–B2

White would have lost material to another tactical device, the skewer, after 3. K–N2 R–R7ch and 4. . . . RxQ. The move chosen, 3. R–B2, allows Black to win with 3. . . . BxRch because 4. KxB R–R7ch 5. B–N2—the only way to seal up the skewer—permits 5. . . . RxBch 6. KxR QxQch, another version of Removing the Defender. (Of course, 4. QxB QxB cuts White's losses, but his two-pawn deficit should eventually cost him the game. Or, rather, should cost her the game—it was a women's tournament.)

3. . . .   Q–N6ch??

Positions with opposite-colored bishops often suggest optical illusions (see Visual Errors, P. 179), and here Black fell into one. The move played appears decisive until you notice 4. K–B1!, which would have turned the game around: *(a)* 4. . . . BxR 5. QxB and the checks are over, leaving White a bishop ahead; *(b)* 4. . . . Q–R5—threatening 5. . . . R–R8ch 6. BxR QxB mate—is met by 5. Q–N2ch P–B3 6. R–K1, permitting the White K to escape by way of K2; and *(c)* the trappy 4. . . . R–R7!? (5. RxR?? Q–N8 mate!), which can be beaten by 5. Q–N2ch.

But White, also suffering from an optical illusion, thought that the kingside pieces would mutually defend one another:

| 4. B–N2?? | BxRch |
| 5. QxB | R–R8ch! |

The pin on White's bishop forces the removal of the defending king—*6. KxR QxQ* and White resigned.

Double Attack

Most beginning players have a recognizable style. They make one threat after another until interrupted by an enemy threat (which they sometimes just ignore). When, by some miracle, they find themselves making two threats with the same move, it is enough to decide the game. I remember making my first knight fork, thinking it was the height of tactical thought.

But double attacks—forks, skewers, etc.—don't just happen; they are made possible by superior piece activity and—on the other side of the board—by carelessness. The latter comes about when you start putting your pieces on unprotected squares. Of course, you can't make any sort of advance with all your pieces in mutual protection. But you can provide insurance against surprises like the following.

Peretz–Saidy, Netanya 1969
Black to play

Black hasn't completed his development and can't play the natural . . . P–QN4 and . . . B–N2 until his QR moves off the long diagonal. Moreover, Black dislikes 1. . . . R–QN1 because of 2. Q–Q6! QxQ 3. RxQ, after which his problems remain (3. . . . B–Q2 4. RxB is impossible, and 3. . . . P–QN4 runs into trouble after 4. KR–Q1 followed by N–R5). So . . .

1. . . .   **R–R2**

Black was probably counting on 2. Q–Q6 QxQ 3. RxQ P–QN4 followed by . . . B–Q2 (protected now by the R at QR2) or . . . R–K1–K2–B2.

2. Q–Q4ch

White wins a rook with the double attack.

Superior piece activity is another matter. Since both sides normally have weaknesses, the player with the most efficient and coordinated force will be able to exploit its advantage tactically.

Keres–Mikenas, Moscow 1954
Black to move

In the diagramed position, Black has obtained a fine game in the opening *(1. P–K4 P–QB4 2. N–KB3 N–QB3 3. P–Q4 PxP 4. NxP N–B3 5. N–QB3 P–Q3 6. B–QB4 P–K3 7. O–O B–K2 8. B–N3 O–O 9. B–K3 B–Q2 10. P–B4 NxN 11. BxN B–B3 12. Q–Q3 P–QN4! 13. P–QR3 P–QR4 14. P–K5 PxP 15. PxP N–Q2)* using tactics such as removal of the defender—16. NxP NxP! 17. BxN QxQ 18. PxQ BxN favors Black who has many weak pawns to attack. The diagram was reached with *16. Q–K3 P–N5 17. PxP PxP 18. N–K2.*

18. . . .   **R–R4!**

Up to now the position has deceptively appeared to favor White's pieces, which seem more aggressively placed. But White, one of the finest tacticians of the twentieth century, realized that Black had more than equalized. He knew that the weakness of his KP and the difference in scope of the two white-square bishops gave Black the advantage.

But a red light should have lit up in his field of vision after 18. . . . R–R4. That move seemed only to be a solid way of pressuring the KP and preparing to take over the QR-file with 19. . . . Q–R1. White failed to make the connection between Black's increasing piece activity and its tactical exploitation.

19. P–B3?   **BxP!**

The White KN2 square didn't seem to be a target, but suddenly Black's activity makes it one. Now 20. KxB Q–R1ch and 21. . . . RxR would have won quickly. White managed to play on with dignity for thirty moves after *20. PxP BxP 21. RxR BxR(8)!* *22. R–N5 BxN 23. RxB*, but his position was already beyond repair.

Faulty Tactics

Black's last sequence is what we call a "little" combination, although it takes a bit of hard calculation. One or two tactical devices stand out, and the rest of it is "if he plays there, I play there." Masters make it look routine. Tactical play, however, is a double-edged sword, no matter how familiar you are with forks, skewers, and other tactical devices.

Euwe–Unzicker, Dusseldorf 1951—*1. P–Q4 N–KB3 2. P–QB4 P–K3 3. N–QB3 B–N5 4. Q–B2 P–B4 5. PxP 0–0 6. P–QR3 BxBP 7. N–B3 N–B3 8. P–K3 P–Q4 9. P–QN4 B–Q3 10. B–N2 P–QR4 11. P–N5 N–K4 12. PxP PxP 13. B–K2 B–K3 14. NxN BxN 15. P–B4 B–Q3 16. 0–0 B–QB4 17. Q–Q3 B–KN5*

Here it is Black, the player who seeks to exploit White's weaknesses tactically, making the critical error. His last move clears the K-file and prepares to take aim at K6. There is a threat to build up slowly with 18. . . . R–K1. There is also a tactical trick in Black's mind. If White's knight moves Black might play 18. . . . BxPch 19. QxB R–K1 with the familiar skewer along the file.

But one of the pitfalls to tactical play is the failure to notice indirect means of defense. For example, how does 18. N–R4 defend against the skewer trick? Black doesn't look for an answer.

18. N–R4	BxPch??
19. QxB	R–K1
20. B–K5!	Resigns

Another trap is thinking you are the only player who can use tactics:

Ozola–Fishman, Riga 1977—*1. P–K4 P–QB3 2. P–Q3 P–Q4 3. N–Q2 P–KN3 4. P–KN3 B–N2 5. B–N2 N–KB3 6. P–K5 N–N5 7. P–Q4 P–KR4 8. P–KR3 N–KR3 9. N–N3 B–B4 10. P–KB3 N–R3 11. P–N4 B–Q2 12. B–B1 Q–N3 13. B–K2 P–QB4 14. QPxP Q–B2 15. P–KB4 NxBP 16. QxP*

Here Black could have gotten a reasonable position with 16. . . . NxN and 17. . . . PxP. But he wanted to humiliate White's pieces now that the center was opened. Black played *16. . . . N–K5* in preparation for 17. . . . N–N6. The main point was "if 17. QxN then 17. . . . B–QB3 skewering queen and rook." But White simply played *17. QxN! B–QB3* and forced resignation with *18. Q–B4!*. One faulty skewer deserves one good pin.

And the fragility of one's piece placement can also unhinge your tactical design.

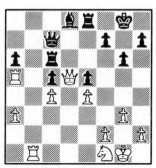

Byrne–Kavalek, Sousse 1967
White to move

White's position has the cosmetic appearance of activity. Actually his rook is about to be exiled on QR4, and his queen is threatened with . . . B–B3 and . . . R–Q1. The desperate urge to overcome a rapidly declining position must have contributed to what now happens.

1. RxRP!?   **RxR**
2. R–N7

Can White really be better? He certainly would be after 2. . . . Q–B1 3. QxPch and probably would be after 2. . . . QxR 3. QxQ

RxP 4. N–K3 and 5. N–Q5. White's clever skewer along the seventh rank seems to have saved him.

2. . . .   **R–Q3!**

But White's pieces hang together so fragilely that any disruption is fatal. Black's 2. . . . R–Q3 wins a rook safely (3. RxQ RxQ 4. KPxR BxR), and thus gives White's house-of-cards position the final shove.

"And with a Little Pin"

". . . bores through his castle-wall, and farewell king." That's the way Shakespeare's Richard II describes the fate of real monarchs. But the chess pin can have the same impact on wooden kings—as well as on bishops, rooks, knights, and queens.

Beginners learn quickly to avoid the elementary pins, such as leaving your queen at K2 in front of your king when your opponent can pin one to another with R–K1 along the open file. But pins, because of their number in a typical game, can be confusing to anyone. You may see one pin developing, think you are getting out of it easily, and then walk into a newly created one.

Polugaevsky–Hort, Manila 1975
White to move

White has permitted a relatively harmless pin on his rook (1. R–B1?? QxQ). He could get out of it with 1. R–Q7 but that would enable Black to defend (1. . . . R–K8ch 2. K–R2 QxQch 3. RxQ R–K3) or counterattack (3. . . . R–K7). Probably best here is "luft" with 1. P–N3 (see First-rank Failure), which gives White's king a good flight square and deprives Black's queen of the KB5 square once the White pieces get off the QN8–KR2 diagonal.

1. Q–Q7??

This seems quite natural—getting out of the pin and threatening KB7.

1. . . .	R–K8ch!
2. K–R2	R–QB8

But there is suddenly a new pin—to the White king not to the queen. White's rook is attacked twice and cannot be protected again. He resigned shortly.

There is no magical method of dealing with pins except to recognize and anticipate them. Recognition isn't easy, as the last example attests. In that case White had to foresee the lining up of his king and rook along what appears to be a safely blocked diagonal. In the next example Black loses material because of a tricky pin that is virtually invisible.

Krogius–Geller, Leningrad 1960
Black to move

Where is the exploitable pin? Black didn't see one and played *1. . . . K–N1*, preparing to double rooks along the QB-file. All his pieces and pawns are defended adequately, it seems.

White's surprise was *2. NxP!*, which not only wins a pawn but destroys Black's castled protection. The trick involves two tactical devices. After 2. . . . QxN 3. R–QR3 the Black NP is pinned to its queen. And the queen cannot retreat because of a skewer. What is being skewered is not another unit of material but a square—a mating square (3. . . . Q–N3 4. R–R8 mate).

The pin and skewer together led to Black's collapse (*2 . . . KR–QB1 3. QxP RxP 4. P–QR3—luft!—K–R2 5. R–QN3 K–R3 6. B–N7ch Black resigns*).

This kind of surprise pin can only be anticipated by a good sense of danger. "Where are the potential pins?" "If I'm pinned along that file (diagonal, rank), how easy is it to get out?" These are the questions to ask yourself. And they would be enough— if pins were the only thing to worry about during a game. But let's see how a pin is permitted by a good player.

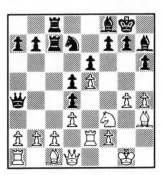

Dely–Hort, Sarajevo 1964
Black to play

There's an old baseball story in which a veteran player asks his colleague: "Suppose you're pitching against Mickey Mantle with the bases loaded, two out, and a count of two strikes and one ball. What do you throw?" The colleague interrupts: "Hold on. How did I get the two strikes and the ball?" In other words, what I do now is a product of what I did before. My past successes and failures indicate my future strategy.

There is a history to this position, too, and it had a strong influence on Black. White had begun a kingside attack by first closing off the center (P–K5) and advancing his pawns (P–KR4 and P–KN4). To obtain the necessary counterplay, Black put a knight on Q5, encouraged White to capture it, and then recapture with a pawn on QB4. This opened the QB-file from Black's side of the board and made it difficult for White to shield himself with P–B3.

Black's whole strategy has been to assault the QB7 target. If he can capture the White QBP, his rooks (and the bishop temporarily entombed at KR2) will spring to life. But should he play 1. . . . RxP?

It's a good policy to think hard before making such a move, the kind that wins material or otherwise changes the balance of the position. Black sees that after 1. . . . RxP he will be temporarily pinned along the Q8–QR5 diagonal. Therefore he has to satisfy himself first that the pin cannot be exploited.

Black's thoughts probably went something like this: "He can work on the pin with 2. N–K1. But then I have 2. . . . RxR! 3. QxQ RxRch 4. K–N2 N–B4 followed by 5. . . . NxQP with a tremendous game. (In this case the pin doesn't really pin.) Or, after 1. . . . RxP White could play 2. P–N3 (another way of exploiting Black's pieces: removal of the defender and fork, 2. . . . Q–B3 3. NxP), but this is OK for me also: 2. P–N3 Q–B3 3. NxP RxB!; e.g., 4. RxR QxR or 4. NxQ RxQch 5. RxR RxN. Finally, he could just simplify down with 2. RxR QxR 3. QxQ RxQ 4. NxP, but after 4. . . . R–B1 he must lose either the KP or QP."

Thus satisfied Black played *1. . . . RxP* and threatened 2. . . . BxP 3. QxB RxBch. But White turned the game around with *2. B–B4!*.

Now Black's predicament becomes clear. He cannot get out of the pin (2. . . . Q–B3 3. NxP) but must do something about such threats as 3. N–K1 and 3. P–N3. The pin could be exploited immediately after 1. . . . RxP, but it wasn't going to disappear. As Hort said later, "Don't hurry to stick your head into a noose."

A final example of the insidiousness of pins is Menchik–Alatortsev, Moscow 1935—*1. N–KB3 P–Q4 2. P–Q4 N–KB3 3. P–B4 P–B3 4. PxP PxP 5. N–B3 N–B3 6. B–B4 P–QR3 7. P–K3 B–B4 8. R–B1 R–B1 9. B–Q3 BxB 10. QxB P–K3 11. 0–0 B–K2 12. P–KR3 0–0 13. KR–Q1?! N–QR4! 14. N–K5 N–B5 15. Q–K2 Q–R4 16. N–Q3 P–QN4! 17. N–B5 BxN 18. PxB RxP 19. P–QN3 KR–B1 20. PxN RxP*. Black has created pin #1 on White's QN.

Position after 20. . . . RxP

If there was no QRP White could defend with 21. N–R2, a simple unpinning idea that occurs quite frequently. And if there was no KP white could play 21. N–N1, since the QB on KB4 would defend the R on QB1. But as things are, White needs an ingenious idea, or he will lose the material edge.

The right way to get out of the pin is 21. B–K5 so that on 21. . . . N–Q2 White plays 22. NxQP! Then the pin turns out to be insufficiently pinning (22. . . . RxR 23. N–K7ch K–B1 24. NxR RxN 25. B–N2 or 22. . . . PxN 23. Q–N4 NxB 24. QxRch!).

| 21. P–K4? | RxN |
| 22. B–Q2? | |

This was White's trick, meeting pin #1 with pin #2. (Actually the best defense is 22. RxR RxR 23. PxP PxP 24. B–K5 R–B5 25. BxN. And the best winning try by Black after 22. RxR would be 22. . . . QxR 23. R–QB1 QxRch! 24. BxQ RxBch and 25. . . . NxP.)

| 2. . . . | QxP! |

And here is pin #3. White can't unravel her pieces and has to permit Black a two-pawn advantage. She resigned after 23. *RxR* (23. R–R1 Q–B5 24. QxQ R[6]xQ) 23. . . . . *RxR 24. PxP NxP 25. Q–N4 R–B5 26. Q–N3 R–B1 27. B–K3 Q–N6!*

Overlooking or Overestimating Checks

Checks are the most common tactical device simply because they are the most forcing of moves. A threat to your queen or a

capture of a piece may sometimes be ignored. But not a check.
And since checks are so much a part of the game they are often
taken for granted—and overlooked. Even by the best players:

Keene–Botvinnik, Hastings 1966/67
Black to move

A former world champion is the victim of this time. As Black
he had mishandled what half a dozen moves before was an overwhelming position. He would now like to play 1. . . . R–B7 but
sees that White may draw with checks beginning with 2. Q–K6ch.
Having seen that danger, one would think Black would be well
aware of other checking dangers. But, discouraged by the change
in his fortunes, he played:

1. . . .	**RxN??**
2. Q–N4ch	**Resigns**

Checks add force to any of the tactical tricks—such as a double
attack in this case—that we've already considered. The tricks may
be disguised, as in the following:

Bronstein–Taimanov, Baku 1961—*1. P–K4 P–QB4 2. N–KB3
P–K3 3. P–Q4 PxP 4. NxP N–QB3 5. N–QB3 Q–B2 6. B–K3
P–QR3 7. P–QR3 P–QN4 8. NxN QxN 9. B–K2 B–B4 10. B–Q4!
P–B3? 11. BxNP! PxB 12. Q–R5ch P–N3 13. QxB and White won.*

Black didn't like 10. . . . N–B3 because of 11. P–K5!; e.g., 11.
. . . QxP 12. B–B3 or 11. . . . BxB 12. QxB QxP 13. 0–0–0. But in de-
ciding to play 10. . . . P–B3 he should have considered the possible

dangers of opening up a checking line to his king. He could discount 11. B–R5ch as a danger, but this false sense of security led to the loss of a vital pawn.

The last example was a double attack using a check. Another is the removal of the defender using a check. Here's an ancient example.

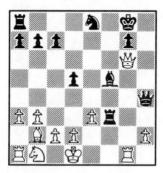

Williams–Lowenthal, London 1851
White to move

In this, one of the earliest tournament games ever played, White must choose a retreat square for his queen. The passive retreat to KN2 is unattractive because it walks into . . . B–K5 followed by . . . R–B7. The more forcing 1. Q–N5 at least offers to trade queens and reduce the Black attacking army.

After lengthy thought—and in those days, thought was usually measured in hours, not minutes—White played *1. Q–N5??* and collapsed after *1. . . . R–B8ch.* White must either play 2. RxR, leaving his queen unprotected, or permit mate, 2. K–K2 Q–B7 mate.

On the other hand, not all checks are good. In a typical game of forty moves the opportunity to check arises more than fifty times—sometimes more. But you rarely see more than ten checks per game. Most of the available checks deserve the German name *wopatzerschach*—"a check so bad that only a patzer would give it."

Keres–Mikenas, Buenos Aires 1939
Black to move

White, a pawn behind, has excellent compensation in view of his control of the king file and potential mating threats. If Black retreats his queen to QB1, he is mated by QxBP and Q–N7. If the queen grabs the QP, White mates with Q–K8ch.

1. . . .   **Q–B4ch??**

Well, why not give a check? You get the initiative (for a move) and feel like the aggressor.

2. K–R1

But the feeling is short-lived. Black has no followup to his first check (2. . . . N–B7ch 3. BxN) and no inexpensive method of answering White's threat of 3. Q–K8ch RxQ 4. RxR mate. Black had to play *2. . . . B–K4* to stay alive, but he could have quietly resigned after *3. PxB*.

Sometimes a move like 1. . . . Q–B4ch is described as a "spite check," a last burst of aggression before resigning. However, there was no reason for such pessimism. With 1. . . . QxQ! 2. RxQ B–Q3 Black has excellent chances—not just to draw but to win. After 3. R–K1 B–B1! Black exchanges down to a safe pawn-ahead ending. And after 3. R–Q7 R–K1! Black takes over the open file with this own threat of mate on the last rank.

Checks are valuable if you recognize their true value. Over-estimating your own checks or underestimating your opponent's is another critical error. In the next example White over- and underestimates.

Suttles–Minic, Palma 1970
White to move

White must defend, and that means giving up the Exchange for one of the enemy bishops. The time is now—1. RxB QxR, and now 2. Q–B7ch or 2. Q–N5! with threats of perpetual check should draw.

1. Q–B7ch   **K–R1**

White can still draw by maintaining his checks—2. Q–N8ch K–R2 3. Q–B7ch K–N3 4. Q–N3ch. Black may even lose by missing a double attack (3. . . . K–R3?? 4. Q–B4ch).

2. RxB??

But White plays to win, thinking that after 2. . . . QxR he can win the bishop with an all-important check (3. Q–N8ch! K–R2 4. QxBch). What he overlooks is that Black can play this game as well:

2. . . . *Q–R8ch!* 3. *K–B2 Q–B6ch* 4. *K–K1 QxNch* 5. *K–B1 Q–B6ch* 6. *K–K1 Q–K6ch* 7. *K–B1 B–R3ch,* and Black must win the rook and keep his extra piece.

Special Cases: First-rank Failure

Some tactical situations based on recurring piece placements deserve special attention. The simplest to foresee and easiest to prevent is a mate by rook or queen on an unobstructed first rank. And any player who claims he's never been victimized by this beginner's nemesis is probably lying.

My first humiliating chess experience went like this: I was twelve years old and had just read all the books on the game at the local library. This convinced me I was a likely candidate for imminent grandmastership. One day a thirteen-year-old neighbor challenged me to a game, and I felt confident. He had played more than I had but read less, and as the game progressed I could tell I was the better player.

And I would have won, too. I grabbed a pawn and then a knight, and after about twenty-five moves there must have been a hundred ways to win—and only one to lose. As I began to finish him off I dropped a rook to the seventh rank—"the absolute seventh rank" that I had seen recommended in some book. But the book didn't mention much about first ranks. He played R–QN8ch and my king, confined to the rank by pawns in front of it, was mated.

Inexperienced players tend to go through a progression. After a few games they learn that castling is a very important move. But after castling in a few games they find their king getting mated along an unprotected first rank. Then they try playing P–KR3 or P–KN3 as soon as they castle—but this just leads to kingside weaknesses and new mates. About this time in their playing career they discover that chess isn't as easy a game as it first appears.

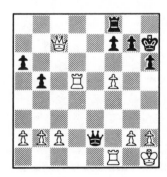

White to move

One of the hard lessons to learn is how to worry about a position. In this game from the 1977 U.S. Open, White, who went by the name of Sneaky Pete, had been winning for several moves. He should take some extra precautions just to insure his victory. There was no reason to hurry. But he didn't worry enough:

1. KR–Q1	R–K1
2. QxP	Q–K8ch
3. RxQ	RxR mate

Was Sneaky Pete embarrassed? Not at all. He was a computer.

Make Luft, Not War

The two methods of avoiding first-rank failure are relatively easy. If you have the time and means—as Sneaky Pete did—simply play P–KR3 or P–KN3 gaining "luft," German for "air." Your king now has an escape square. (P–KB3 often weakens the castled position too much by exposing a diagonal to the KN1 square.)

When this isn't available—usually because you can't spare a move for luft—the remedy is simple awareness. When an average or better player is victimized by his first rank, you can blame his or her failure to look out for the danger.

And even luft is insufficient if the King's flight square is under attack. Who would have guessed that two moves following the next diagram White would be lost because of a first-rank fiasco?

Korchnoi–Levenfish, Moscow 1953
Black to move

White will regain his pawn on K4 and have winning chances because of the weak enemy pawns on the queenside. Black might try to give White a weak pawn too by playing 1. . . . P–K6 2. RxP RxR. But White can answer 3. QxR! QxNP? 4. Q–K7!, and it is Black's first rank that decides the game.

1. . . .	**B–B1**
2. BxP	**B–R6!?**

Black's last is a trappy move. The White first rank is vulnerable since the KN2 flight square is covered now by the bishop. This is hardly fatal, but it places an onus of accuracy on White. With a clear head he can win a pawn with 3. QxP! (3. . . . KR–N1 4. Q–B3 RxP 5. QxQ PxQ 6. R–Q6, or 3. . . . QR–N1 4. B–N2!! RxQ 5. RxR mate; 4. . . . RxRch 5. RxR threatening 6. BxB and 6. QxRch).

White has other good moves, such as 3. Q–KB3. Even the humble 3. B–N2 keeps some of his advantage. But not 3. R–Q6, an attractive alternative.

3. R–Q6??	**RxB!**
4. RxR	**QxR**

This is the kind of complication White never expected. (He may have seen 3. . . . RxB 4. RxQ RxR mate but assumed that 4. RxR would remove all dangers.) White's sense of danger simply wasn't directed to the first rank.

Since 5. R–K8ch RxR 6. PxQ R–K8 is still mate, White played 5. *QxP*, but after 5. . . . *QxP!* (rubbing it in) 6. *Q–K1 P–N3!* he had to resign. It turned out that White's last hope was the vulnerability of Black's first rank. Once that hope was dashed, Black's extra piece had to win.

Mishandling Long Diagonals

Although first-rank mates have haunted players since the Arab traders brought the game to Europe, there is another common tactical problem—built into typical middlegames—that is relatively new. This occurs when a player weakens his long diagonal, the lines that run from QR1 to KR8 and KR1 to QR8. They crop up nowadays because many players fianchetto their bishops (that is, develop them at N2). This development is an attempt to exploit the diagonal, but it may also turn out to be a weakening of the diagonal:

Kochiev–Ivanov, U.S.S.R. 1976—*1. N–KB3 N–KB3 2. P–KN3 P–Q4 3. B–N2 P–K3 4. 0–0 B–K2 5. P–Q3 P–QN3 6. QN–Q2 B–N2 7. P–K4 PxP 8. PxP NxP?? 9. N–K5! Black resigns.*

Black concedes because he will lose a piece. Probably he had counted on 9. . . . N–B4 (or 9. . . . N–Q3) 10. BxB NxB. But his long diagonal is still weak—11. Q–B3! with a double attack at KB7 and QN7. And if Black plays 9. . . . NxN instead, he will lose a piece to 10. BxB.

This diagonal disaster came about because Black, though aware of the dangers, calculated them poorly. In the next case Black was completely unaware of them.

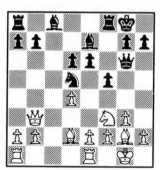

Averbakh–Ragozin, Moscow 1954
Black to move

After White's spirited opening play *(1. P–QB4 P–KB4 2. P–KN3 N–KB3 3. B–N2 P–K3 4. N–KB3 B–K2 5. 0–0 0–0 6. P–Q4 P–Q3 7. N–B3 Q–K1 8. R–K1 N–K5 9. Q–B2 Q–N3 10. B–K3 NxN 11. QxN N–Q2 12. P–B5! N–B3 13. PxP PxP 14. Q–N3! N–Q4 15. B–Q2)*, Black has some queenside weaknesses and an immediate problem of completing his development. He would like to bring his QB out, but 15. . . . B–Q2 16. QxP is unpleasant.

The natural method of protecting his QNP is 15. . . . P–N3, since 15. . . . R–N1 commits a rook to a clumsy square and may

leave the QRP hanging in the future. But 15. . . . P–N3 is a bad
mistake. •

15. . . .	P–N3?
16. B–N5!	

White threatens to bring his long diagonal to life with 17. BxB
NxB 18. N–K5! PxN 19. BxR. Black may not have been blind to
the dangers along the diagonal but probably thought that his
blockading knight on Q4 would hold the line. Now, if he plays
16. . . . R–N1, White wins material with 17. BxB NxB 18. Q–R3!,
striking at QR7 and Q6.

16. . . .	BxB
17. NxB	B–N2

Black didn't like 17. . . . QxN because 18. BxN would cost a
pawn (18. . . . PxB 19. QxPch and QxR), and he had to do something about the threats of 18. BxN and 18. NxKP BxN 19. BxN.
Now, after 17. . . . B–N2, it seems that his diagonal has finally
been neutralized.

18. P–K4!

This, however, decides the game from a positional point of
view. Black ends up with two highly vulnerable center pawns:
18. . . . PxP 19. NxP(4) N–K2 (to meet the threat of 20. N–B3)
*20. NxP BxB 21. QxPch! QxQ 22. RxQ B–R6 23. RxN QR–Q1 24.
N–K4 RxP 25. QR–K1 P–KR3 26. RxP R–B1 27. P–B3 R–B7? 28.
N–B6ch! Black resigns.* It ends with a first-rank mate.

Mistakes with Pieces

"Whenever I move a piece, it's a tactical error," complained the beginner. "And whenever I move a pawn, it's a positional error. What should I do?"

"Move something else," said the master.

If only it was that simple. You have to move something: only in contract bridge can you "pass." But chess is hard enough with the variety of faulty piece moves.

Mishandling your pieces is the fastest way to give your opponent tactical chances. At any given moment you may have as many as a hundred different possible moves with your queen, rooks, king, knights, and bishops. Only 10 percent of those possibilities are likely to be good moves. The rest are either mediocre, or just plain bad.

Faulty Development

Development is better than riches. With your pieces developed you can take middlegame risks and engage in long-term planning. Without development, you have to worry about getting out of the opening alive.

Yes, there are many opening systems in use that sacrifice development for strategic pawn moves or pawn-grabbing. But these systems require extra care and may be intrinsically unsound even in the hands of the best players.

Geller–Petrosian, U.S.S.R. 1963—*1. P–K4 P–K3 2. P–Q4 P–Q4 3. N–QB3 B–N5 4. P–K5 P–QN3 5. N–B3 Q–Q2 6. B–Q2 B–B1!? 7. P–QR4 N–QB3 8. B–K2 KN–K2 9. 0–0*

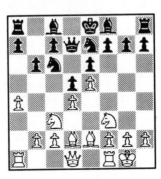

Position after 9. 0–0

Black's delay in development is risky but far from fatal. His undeveloping 6th move is aimed at avoiding the exchange of his good bishop (6. . . . P–QB4? 7. N–QN5). With the center closed Black can afford such exotic ideas. But . . .

9. . . .	**P–B3?**
10. R–K1	**PxP?**

Black can't afford to open the game up so early. He would be ready for the . . . P–B3 break only after 9. . . . B–N2, 10. . . . P–KR3, and 11. . . . 0–0–0. But in the current position he mistakenly feels he is ensuring against danger by taking the initiative in the center (11. PxP N–N3 12. B–KB1 B–N2 followed by . . . 0–0–0 or . . . B–K2 and . . . 0–0).

11. B–QN5!

Surprises like this come naturally when you have several potential weaknesses (the center, the KB2 square) and virtually no development. Now Black would be swallowed alive after 11. . . . P–K5 12. N–K5 Q–Q3 13. B–KB4 or 11. . . . PxP 12. KNxP Q–Q3 13. NxN NxN 14. B–KB4 Q–Q2 15. QxP!.

11. . . .	**N–N3**
12. NxKP	**KNxN**
13. RxN	**P–QR3**

This concedes a pawn or two and eventually the game *(14. BxN QxB 15. NxP B–Q2 16. B–N5 B–Q3 17. Q–R5ch! K–B1 18. Q–B3ch K–N1 19. RxP)*, but Black is already too far behind (13. . . . B–K2 14. Q–B3 B–B3 15. NxP! BxR 16. N–B6ch!; 14. . . . B–N2 15. QR–K1; or 13. . . . B–Q3 14. RxPch!).

Most players know how to develop once they've played their first dozen games. But they still make development errors of a great variety. For example, they delay development even in open positions for sophisticated tactical or strategic reasons:

Portisch–Bronstein, Monaco 1969—*1. P–Q4 P–Q4 2. P–QB4 P–QB4 3. BPxP N–KB3 4. P–K4!? NxKP 5. PxP NxP(4) 6. N–KB3 P–K3 7. N–B3*

Here White provides for a slight initiative because of his restrictive pawn on Q5. Black can exchange that pawn off but at the cost of developing his opponent's game. The most promising continuation is 7. . . . B–K2 8. B–K3 Q–R4 with . . . 0–0 and later . . . R–Q1.

But in this game Black played *7. . . . PxP?! 8. QxP!*, and to avoid the exchange of queens that favors White (8 . . . N–B3 9. QxQch NxQ 10. N–Q5) he chose the clumsy *8. . . . Q–K2ch? 9. B–K3 N–B3 10. B–QN5 B–Q2 11. 0–0 N–K3*. This procedure not only encourages White's development (9. B–K3) but inhibits Black's by keeping his KB at home. Black couldn't even castle queenside (11. . . . 0–0–0 12. QBxN QxB 13. QxP).

As played, Black never got a chance to castle: *12. N–K5! NxN* (12. . . . 0–0–0 13. BxN BxB 14. NxB!) *13. QxN BxB 14. NxB P–QR3 15. QR–Q1! R–Q1 16. B–N6! RxR* (16. . . . PxN 17. BxR NxB 18. QxPch N–B3 19. KR–K1) *17. RxR P–B3 18. Q–KB5 P–N3 19. N–B7ch K–B2* (19. . . . NxN 20. Q–B8ch and R–Q7) *20. Q–Q5 Black resigns.*

Only slightly better than no development is *faulty development*. Simply bringing the pieces out from the first rank may permit you to castle quickly and avoid a catastrophe like Black's above. But the opening eventually comes to an end and you have to begin planning a middlegame strategy. The placement of your pieces has a great deal to do with that planning.

For example, this message has often been handed down to beginners as if engraved on tablets from Mt. Sinai: "Develop your knights before your bishops." This is a simplistic way to put a handy bit of wisdom. The reasoning goes something like this: after the initial pawn moves you must first develop some minor pieces. But the pawns have not been firmly set in the center at this point. With a fluid center, you want knights out rather than bishops because knights can be more flexibly adapted to changed circumstances. Bishops, once developed, often get kicked around by enemy center pawns. For illustration:

Korchnoi–Szabo, Bucharest 1954

1. P–QB4	P–K4
2. N–QB3	N–KB3
3. P–KN3	B–B4?

Had White already committed himself in the center with P–K4, or made P–K3 and P–Q4 difficult to enforce, this would be a good square on which to post the bishop. After 3. . . . N–B3 4. P–K4?! B–B4 for instance, Black has excellent piece play. But watch how Black's pieces, beginning with this bishop, get smothered now.

4. B–N2	0–0
5. P–K3!	R–K1
6. KN–K2	N–B3
7. 0–0	P–Q3
8. P–Q4	B–N3

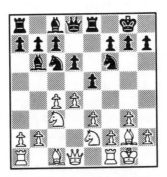

Position after 8. . . . B–N3

Black's pieces only appear to be well off. Now he continues with classical development (posting knights on B3, bishops on B4) and is overrun by more accurate play: *9. P–KR3 B–KB4 10. P–Q5 N–N1 11. P–KN4! B–Q2 12. N–N3 P–KR3 13. K–R2 P–QR4 14. P–B4 PxP 15. PxP N–R2 16. P–N5! N–R3* (16. . . . PxP 17. PxP NxP 18. Q–R5 P–KB3 19. BxN and 20. B–K4) *17. PxP Q–R5?! 18. PxP N–B3 19. P–B5! B–K6 20. QN–K4! NxN 21. NxN BxB 22. RxB N–B4* (22. . . . RxN 23. BxR QxB 24. Q–R5 wins since White avoids perpetual check with 24. . . . Q–K4ch 25. K–R1 Q–K5ch 26. R–B3) *23. Q–N4! RxN 24. BxR QxQ 25. PxQ NxB 26. P–B6! R–K1 27. QR–K1 N–B4 28. RxRch BxR 29. R–K1 B–R5 30. R–K3 Black resigns.*

Notice that Black's KB came alive later in the game, but to the detriment of his other pieces. White's QB never seemed to be doing much either, but it was well posted at QB1 in support of the kingside advance. That advance turned out remarkably. R–KR3–R8 was the key final threat.

The Offsides Piece

Once the pieces are developed they can be *un*developed by being sent off to a side of the board or to a theater of action from which it's difficult to extract them. Being offsides isn't a hanging offense per se. Often the knights are excellently posted on QR5 or KR4, for example. The queen's exile to one corner of the board may be more than compensated for by the inhibiting impact it exerts on the enemy pieces.

But more often than not these are misplacements. A knight on the R-file can control a maximum of four squares, compared with eight if posted in the center. A rook may not only suffer from diminished scope but semipermanent entombment on the board's rim. And a queen's adventures may be triply damaging: *(1)* because its absence from a critical sector may create a vast imbalance of forces there, *(2)* because the queen may be subject to harassing attacks from lesser pieces that grant the enemy time for other pursuits, and *(3)* because the queen may even get trapped.

The rook and bishop seem to be less prone to misplacement than queen and knight. But any piece can be trapped anywhere, including in the center of the board. Close attention is vital since a general rule ("Never put a piece on the side of the board") would be impossible to follow.

Vogt–Berndt, Berlin 1936
White to move

Is there any difference in mobility between the two rooks here? Very little. Black's is slightly better placed, but that is temporary and has more to do with the kings than the rooks. Black's rook prevents the White king from cooperating in the defense of his kingside pawns. White would like to use his own rook to the same effect, so . . .

1. R–R5??

Now on 1. . . . K–N3 2. R–K5 K–B3 3. R–R5 White is ready to accept a draw through repetition of position. Black's king cannot advance and his rook has few immediate targets. But Black ends the game with:

1. . . .	P–N3!
2. RxP	

The only move to save a rook. However . . .

2. . . .	K–N2.

A rook is such a clumsy piece that it rarely gets an opportunity to go roaming until the later stages of the game. The bishops usually serve best from the wings of the board. They rarely become trapped unless they are caught behind enemy lines.

Perhaps the most famous incident of this, the Bishop Murder Case, occurred in the very first game of the Fischer–Spassky match. The American captured the world champion's pawn on KR2 with his bishop. At the time there were only bishops, pawns, and kings left on the board. Spassky played P–KN3 and the bishop's retreat along the line it had just used was now shut. There was also a Spassky pawn on KB2 to prevent escape along the other line (KN1–QR7). Fischer knew of the dangers in playing this self-exiling bishop capture but had miscalculated his attempt to extricate it. And Spassky led the match 1–0.

A more complicated example of this:

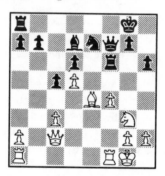

Timman–Najdorf, Reykjavik 1976
White to move

Black has a slight positional advantage, though it is nothing to write home about. Yet the game is quickly decided by White's carelessness in the next two moves. It's true White miscalculated, but, like Fischer, the error lay just as much in the misplacement of the bishop as in poor calculation.

1. B–R7ch	K–R1
2. N–K4	

This seems quite clever at first appearance. Black can't take the bishop because of 3. NxR double check (and mate next move). Black can't play the rook to a safe unoccupied square either. That leaves 2. . . . RxP, which permits 3. NxQP with advantage to White (3. . . . Q–B3 4. N–K4; 3. . . . Q–B1 4. B–N6!).

This brings up another kind of error, one of attitude. Whenever you see a forcing sequence (a combination) which seems to alter the status of the game, sit on your hands. Take another look before moving. If the move you intend to play is really that good, it won't hurt your chances to make sure it's everything it's cracked up to be. Too many players have destroyed a good position with what they considered to be the winning move because they played too quickly.

2. . . .	**P–KN3!**

In his rush to turn the tables White overlooked the fact that his bishop was permanently trapped. His error was also a product of faulty *assumption*, thinking that Black had to move the attacked rook.

After 3. NxR QxN 4. BxP NxB White had theoretical equality of material. But the minor pieces usually make a much faster contribution to the course of the game than a rook and pawn. As the game came to favor Black more and more, White became desperate: 5. QR–K1 R–KN1 6. K–R1 N–R5 7. P–N3 N–B4 8. Q–Q3 Q–B2 9. R–B2 N–K2! 10. P–B4 N–B4 11. R(B)–K2 P–QN4 12. Q–B3ch R–N2 13. R–K6!? BxR 14. PxB Q–N2ch 15. K–N1 N–Q5 16. K–B2 PxP 17. P–B5 NxP 18. Q–B6 N–K2 White resigns.

One of the most graphic punishments of bishop-wandering was Winter–Capablanca, Hastings 1919. After 1. P–K4 P–K4 2. N–KB3 N–QB3 3. N–B3 N–B3 4. B–N5 B–N5 5. 0–0 0–0 6. BxN QPxB 7. P–Q3 B–Q3 8. B–N5 P–R3! 9. B–R4?, White permitted his bishop to be snowed under: 9. . . . P–B4 10. N–Q5 P–KN4! 11. NxNch (11. NxNP NxN) QxN 12. B–N3 B–KN5 13. P–KR3 BxN 14. QxB QxQ 15. PxQ P–KB3. Although Black's bishop was no beauty, at least it could move. The threat of activating the Black bishop on the queenside led to a quick downfall: 16. K–N2 P–QR4 17. P–QR4 K–B2 18. R–R1 K–K3 19. P–R4 KR–QN1! 20. PxP RPxP 21. P–N3 P–B3 22. R–QR2 P–N4 23. KR–R1 P–B5! 24. RPxP (24. QPxP PxBP 25. PxP R–N5!) PxP(N6) 25. BPxP RxP 26. R–R4 RxP 27. P–Q4 R–N4 28. R–B4 R–N5! 29. RxBP RxQP White resigns. The rook pawn just keeps running now.

A queen's transgressions are most commonly exploited. The advantage of a queen over other pieces is greatly misunderstood.

A queen is much stronger than a rook and bishop in most middlegames because of its mobility not its raw muscle. As a battering ram, two pieces may be more successful since they cannot concentrate the force of two units against one target. But a queen, which combines the bishop's diagonal movement and the rook's horizontal-vertical movement, gets around much faster. Anyone who has tried to bring a clumsy rook to the kingside for attack in a typical middlegame, when it means levitating it to the third or fourth rank and negotiating its way over rough terrain to the castled position, knows why the queen is superior.

Yet the queen can be restricted as easily as a rook:

Portisch–Petrosian, Tel Aviv 1964
White to move

Here's a case of simple superiority of a rook over knight and pawn. But White makes a two-fold mistake. He *misunderstands what it takes to win* and tries for greater material advantage. To accomplish that he *decentralizes his queen*—pardonable if temporary, but it isn't temporary.

1. QxP?

Black's many weaknesses could be exploited simply and directly with 1. Q–B3! followed by a penetration at QR8, QN7, or QB6. For example, 1. . . . P–N3 2. Q–R8ch K–N2 3. R–Q8 wins outright. Or 1. . . . Q–K1 2. Q–N7 N–K2 3. R–Q7.

1. . . .   P–N3!

Now the queen is bottled up for a while. It can't be captured, but its absence alone can dissolve White's substantial advantage. The best bet now would be to bring the rook to the KB-file so as to threaten to win material and free the queen with QxNP. Black would not be able to move his king without dropping material, and it is virtually impossible to do anything with his queen.

2. K–B1?	Q–B2
3. K–N1	Q–K2
4. R–Q6?	P–R4
5. Q–R8	P–R5
6. K–R2	Q–B2
7. P–R5	Q–B7!

The game is only a draw since White's P–KR5 plan has made his KNP vulnerable and created the opportunity for perpetual check. After 8. R–Q8ch K–K2 9. QxN QxPch the checks will go on forever.

Instead, White tried 8. *K–N3, but after 8. . . . Q–B8!* the future course was clear: 9. *R–Q8ch K–K2 10. QxN QxPch 11. K–R2 QxRPch 12. K–N2 Q–N5ch 13. K–B1 Q–B5ch 14. K–K1 Q–K5ch draw.*

Such adventures can occur in the opening as well as endgame. For example, Calvo–Korchnoi, Havana 1966, went *1. P–K4 P–QB4 2. N–KB3 P–K3 3. P–Q4 PxP 4. NxP P–QR3 5. B–Q3 B–B4 6. N–N3 B–R2 7. P–QB4 N–QB3 8. 0–0 Q–R5? 9. N(1)–Q2 KN–K2 10. P–B5! N–K4 11. B–K2 P–QN3 12. P–B4 N(4)–B3 13. N–B4! PxP 14. P–N3 Q–R3 (14. . . . Q–R6 15. B–N4) 15. P–B5 Q–B3 16. PxP QxKP 17. N–Q6ch K–B1 18. B–QB4 Black resigns.* White's harassment of the queen put the steam into his attack.

Uncoordinated, Uncooperative

Once pieces are developed, even on good squares, they can become useless if they cannot cooperate with one another. The pieces may individually stand well, but as part of a team they lack harmony.

This may come about because they are jumbled together in a hodgepodge or strewn about across a wide swath of the board. Even if they appear to harmonize, you may suddenly discover that there are natural limits to what you can accomplish with pieces.

Paulsen–Anderssen, Match 1877
Black to move

In this old game Black has banked on a mating combination to offset his two-pawn deficit. What, he wonders, can White do about 1. . . . N–N6ch 2. PxN R–B3 followed by a rook check on KR3? To stop a mate along the KR-file, it seems that White must sacrifice heavily.

But White has a defense, and it has to do with the mutual protection of pieces. White's pieces don't seem to harmonize any better than Black's. But after *1. . . . N–N6ch?? 2. PxN R–B3* White reveals that Black's army is stretched too far. With *3. R–B2!*, a fairly simple move to find, Black remains a piece behind since 3. . . . QxR permits 4. QxR and mates.

A contrasting form of uncoordination is illustrated by Karpov–Unzicker, Milan 1975, which began with 1. P–K4 P–K4 2. N–KB3 N–QB3 3. B–N5 P–QR3 4. B–R4 N–B3 5. 0–0 B–K2 6. R–K1 P–QN4 7. B–N3 P–Q3 8. P–B3 0–0 9. P–KR3 N–QR4 10. B–B2 P–B4 11. P–Q4 Q–B2 12. QN–Q2 B–Q2 13. N–B1 KR–K1 14. P–Q5 N–N2.

Black's pieces are slightly passive on their current squares. White's also appear passive, but they have a better future. His knights are headed for KN3 and KR2 to support P–KB4 and

N–B5. Black's pieces have a longer journey ahead before they reach respectability. Play continued *15. N(3)–R2 P–N3 16. N–N3 P–B5 17. P–B4 PxP 18. BxP.*

Black was ready to bring his QN to QB4 and redevelop his KB at KN2. But his first concern was White's initiative in the center, which threatened to increase with 19. P–K5. With this in mind, Black played *18. . . . B–KB1.*

Actually, Black's pieces are so jumbled that he needed to sort them out quickly with 18. . . . B–QB1 and 19. . . . N–Q2, followed by . . . B–B1–N2 and . . . N–K4. White exploited Black's slight inaccuracy with *19. B–N5!.*

After that move, Black discovered that his uncoordinated pieces permitted no retreat for his attacked KN. After 19. . . . B–N2 20. R–KB1 Q–Q1 White would pin and win a piece with 21. Q–B3.

Black tried to rescue his knight with *19. . . . B–K2,* hoping for 20. R–KB1 Q–B4ch 21. K–R1 NxQP 22. PxN BxB. But after *20. Q–Q2! B–QB1 21. R–KB1 N–Q2 22. N–N4* he resigned in view of threats such as N–R6ch and Q–KB2.

Ryumin–Capablanca, Moscow 1935
Black to move

Another example points up the need for piece coordination in contrast to piece protection. Black's pieces protect one another but don't coordinate. Still, with White's QNP as a target, Black can create counterplay in this inferior position.

1. . . .   **R–R4?**

A terrible move. Black is not threatening the NP because after 2. . . . NxP 3. NxN RxN White gets a winning position with 4. QxR! BxQ 5. RxR K–B1 6. KR–Q1. The right way to bring the Black pieces into harmony is 1. . . . QR–B1 or 1. . . . Q–N4 (e.g., 1. . . . Q–N4 2. P–N6 Q–QB4!).

2. Q–Q4!

White points out immediately the haphazard arrangement of Black's heavy pieces. His minor pieces protect one another but can be harassed. However, his rooks don't have anything to do with each other, and the queen is off in limbo. Now with 3. Q–N4 or 3. Q–N6 (followed by 4. RxN or 4. QxR) White threatens to end the game immediately.

2. . . .   Q–N4

Now at least the Q and KR are connected (so that on 3. Q–N4 QR–R1 4. RxN NxR 5. QxN Black has 29. . . . BxP).

3. Q–N4   P–QN3?

Another awful move, which prevents his rooks from becoming reconnected with . . . R(4)–R1. Black was in bad shape in any event (3. . . . QR–R1 4. P–B4! Q–K2 5. R–B2 or 5. P–K4).

4. R–Q2!   BxP

Perhaps Black discounted 4. R–Q2, the quiet move, and worried only about 4. RxN. There was nothing else here (4. . . . R–QB1 5. RxN; 4. . . . B–B1 5. KR–Q1 R–R2 6. B–B6). Black lost on time in this hopeless position.

Poor Piece Exchanges

Of the many bad moves to be made, the worst are the kind you can't take back. This means pawn advances (since pawns can't retreat) and exchanges of pieces. When you give up one of your minor pieces for one of your opponent's, you must be sure of several things. First, you don't want to exchange a good piece for an inferior one. Second, you don't want to exchange off pieces of equal value—or even an inferior one for a superior one—if the exchange creates positional or strategic problems (such as leaving your kingside weak or removing your best blockading piece).

Also, you don't want to exchange off pieces, regardless of their relative merit, when you need material on the board to sustain an initiative, to create middlegame options, or take advantage of the enemy's cramped position. Similarly you don't avoid exchanges when it unnecessarily costs you time, confuses your pieces, or permits enemy pieces to remain on dominating squares.

A good example of a bad exchange arises out of *1. P–K4 P–K4 2. N–KB3 N–QB3 3. P–Q4 PxP 4. B–QB4 B–B4 5. 0–0 P–Q3 6. P–B3 B–KN5!? 7. Q–N3? BxN 8. BxPch K–B1*

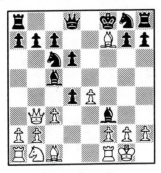

White to move

Black gave up a bishop for a knight at move 7 for a good reason: to weaken the White kingside. But Black is several moves away from taking advantage of this, and after 9. PxB N–B3 (9. . . . N–R4 10. Q–K6) 10. B–Q5 Black has a very good but not won game.

Yet because of the apparent dangers in the position (Black's ability to harass White's only developed pieces with . . . N–K4 or . . . N–R4), White might be coaxed into *9. BxN??* and then *9. . . . RxB 10. PxB*. Although 9. BxN frees White's queen it is doubly bad. It trades off a good *developed* piece for an undeveloped one (and also "develops" Black's rook!). The exchange also eliminates options for White's pieces. For example, after 9. BxN RxB 10. PxB Black has a very strong move in 10. . . . P–KN4!, which prepares to bring the rook to bear with . . . P–N5 or . . .

R–N3–R3. If White played simply 9. PxB he could meet 9. . . . P–N4 with 10. B–R5! threatening 11. Q–B7 mate.

The enormity of Black's advantage after 9. *BxN?? RxB 10. PxB P–KN4!* is shown by two nineteenth-century games. One of them, Reiner–Steinitz, Vienna 1860, went 11. Q–K6 N–K4 12. Q–B5ch K–N2! 13. K–R1 (13. BxP K–R1! 14. P–KB4 N–B6ch) 13. . . . K–R1 14. R–N1 P–N5! 15. P–KB4 (15. PxNP Q–R5) N–B6 16. RxP Q–R5! 17. R–N2 QxPch 18. RxQ R–N8 mate. The other, Kolisch–Anderssen, Paris 1860, went 11. Q–Q1 Q–Q2 12. P–N4 B–N3 13. B–N2 P–Q6! 14. QxP N–K4 15. Q–K2 Q–R6 16. N–Q2 P–N5 and White resigned (17. P–KB4 N–B6ch).

The case of an apparently beneficial exchange turning out badly is illustrated by the following position.

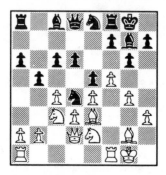

Botvinnik–Tscherbakov, Moscow 1955
White to play

1. B–N5!

This stroke creates grave problems for Black since he has no good response. It's greatest strength, however, is that it forces Black to make a choice. Remember, most mistakes are made when a player is faced with a choice of reasonable alternatives. Here Black sees that 1. . . . Q–B2 allows his KB to be buried by 2. P–B6. White would have a choice himself after 2. . . . B–R1. But it would be a pleasant one, between 3. B–R6 winning material and 3. R–B2, protecting his KBP and preparing to open the KR-file with a subsequent P–KR4–5.

Nor does Black like the looks of 1. . . . P–B3, hemming in his slightly "bad" bishop even more, or 1. . . . N–B3, which sets up a bad pin to be exploited by doubling rooks on the KB-file. Nevertheless, one of these is preferable to:

1. . . .	B–B3?
2. BxB!	NxB
3. NxN	PxN
4. N–K2	Q–N3
5. PxP(5)	RPxP
6. Q–R6!	

In a positional sense, the exchange of black-square bishops can only favor Black. The White bishop is "bad" and Black's knight is available to take up excellent position at K4. The only problem? Black will be mated in a few moves.

The exchange of bishops has left Black with nothing to protect his kingside squares. After 6. . . . N–Q2 White plays 7. P–B6 threatening 8. Q–N7 mate. And if *6. . . . B–Q2*, as played, White wins with 7. *P–N5 N–R4* (7. . . . N–K1 8. R–B4 and 9. R–R4 mates) *8. N–B4 N–N2 9. P–B6*, and on 9. . . . N–K1 10. N–Q5! PxN 11. R–B4 and 12. R–R4.

Some players never like to exchange off pieces because it simplifies the game. They usually end up going into contortions to avoid trades. Then they find out, like White below, that their opponent's pieces are too strong. And that's when the enemy starts to decline exchanges.

Rukavina–Raicevic, Yugoslavia 1975—*1. P–KN3 P–Q4 2. B–N2 P–QB4 3. P–Q3 N–QB3 4. P–QB3 P–KN3 5. N–B3 B–N2 6. 0–0 P–K4 7. P–K4 KN–K2 8. QN–Q2 0–0 9. R–K1 P–KR3 10. PxP NxP 11. N–B4 R–K1 12. P–QR4 N–N3*

Position after 12. . . . N–N3

Black offers to trade off his centralized knight—the one that just came from Q4—for White's useful QB4 knight. That trade would ease the pressure on Black's KP and permit him to complete his development. White, realizing this, begins to self-destruct:

13. N–K3?

This piece just gets in the way of White's KR and QB here. With 13. NxN QxN 14. N–Q2! and N–K4 or N–B4 White would have an excellent game.

13. . . .	N–R4!
14. Q–B2	B–K3

Black now has a slight initiative because of his pressure against the White queenside. He should have maintained it with 15. . . . Q–B2 and 16. . . . QR–Q1 with prospects of . . . P–QB5.

15. N–Q2	Q–Q2?!
16. R–Q1	Q–B2
17. P–N3	QR–Q1
18. N(2)–B4	N–Q4!

There is nothing to gain from a capture on QB5 since White will open up the QN-file (NPxN!) and secure an outpost square at his Q5. Black would much prefer to exchange on his own Q4; e.g., 19. NxN(Q5) BxN 20. BxB RxB 21. NxN QxN, although White would be able to equalize with 22. P–QB4! and 23. B–N2.

White would then have a backward QP, but it could be sufficiently protected while White takes aim at the Black KP.

19. B–Q2?

But White seriously misunderstands the potential dangers of
a middlegame with several minor pieces. Now was the time to
trade. Once Black has eliminated the opening pressure against
his KP, he is ready to take over the initiative by pressuring the
White QP or advancing on the kingside. White's pieces are stuck
in a traffic jam now and this permanently cedes the momentum
to Black.

19. . . .	**N–QB3!**
20. R–K1	**N(4)–K2!**

Black correctly avoids giving White a second chance to trade
pieces. In the next stage Black simply repositioned his pieces
to prepare . . . P–KB4–5 *(21. QR–Q1 K–R2 22. B–QB1 P–B4 23.
N–B1 N–Q4 24. N(1)–K3 N–B3! 25. N–B1 P–B5 26. N(1)–Q2
B–N5 27. N–B3 N–Q4)*, whereas White sought in vain to exchange pieces. Such a positional advantage eventually created
winning tactical ideas.

28. B–N2 Q–B2 (threatening 29. . . . PxP and 30. . . . BxN) *29.
R–KB1 Q–B4! 30. R–Q2 Q–R4 31. Q–Q1?* (sets up a losing pin,
but 31. N–K1 R–KB1 threatening . . . P–B6 and . . . B–R6 was
too painful to bear) *31. . . . N–N3! 32. PxP NxN*, and White resigned in view of 33. NPxN P–K5! winning a piece.

Premature and Postponed Queen Exchanges

The most significant of exchanges is that of queens. Exchanging queens will break the impact of most kingside attacks and
blunt many strategic initiatives in the center and on the queenside. But exchanging queens also emphasizes the importance of
other pieces and turns relatively minor (middlegame) advantages
and weaknesses into endgame monuments. As such, the trade of
queens must be viewed suspiciously. It is rarely neutral. There
is usually some shift of fortunes.

Udovcic–Lilienthal, Moscow 1942—*1. P–K4 P–K4 2. N–KB3 N–QB3 3. B–N5 P–QR3 4. B–R4 N–B3 5. P–Q4 PxP 6. 0–0 B–K2 7. P–K5 N–K5 8. NxP N–B4 9. N–B5 0–0 10. Q–N4 P–KN3 11. BxN QPxB 12. NxBch QxN*

Position after 12. . . . QxN

The exchanges of minor pieces have created a set of dangers for both players. White becomes slightly behind in development and obtains some weak white squares to worry about. Black, however, has *big* problems on the black squares, specifically his KB3 and KR3. White might exploit this in the middlegame or ending, but he can exploit it best only with a queen on the board. With 13. Q–N3! B–B4 14. B–N5 Q–K3 15. N–Q2 he stands very well (15. . . . BxP 16. QR–B1 Q–B4 17. B–K7 or 15. . . . N–K5 16. NxN BxN 17. B–B6 followed by Q–N5–R6).

13. Q–N5?	R–K1
14. R–K1	QxQ
15. BxQ	B–B4

In the ending, Black's only problem is his inability to put a rook on Q1. He can use his minor pieces and queenside pawns very effectively while White tries to catch up in development. And White's KP, so useful in guiding an attack, becomes a target and restricts White's own bishop. The problems are evident after 16. P–QB3 N–Q6 or 16. R–K2 N–Q2 17. P–KB4 P–B3.

| 16. N–R3 | P–QN4 |
| 17. R–K2 | N–R5! |

Black makes steady progress in his plan to create a passed pawn: *18. P–QN3 N–B6 19. R(2)–K1 P–QR4 20. B–Q2 N–K5 21. B–B4 N–B4 22. QR–B1 P–R5! 23. P–QN4 N–R3 24. P–B3 QR–Q1 25. N–B2 BxN! 26. RxB P–QB4 27. P–QR3 P–B5! 28. R–Q2 RxR 29. BxR P–QB4.*

The game ended thematically. *30. PxP NxP 31. R–N1 N–N6 32. B–B4 R–Q1 33. P–R4 R–Q6 34. P–K6 PxP 35. B–K5 P–N5!! 36. BPxP P–B6 37. B–B4 P–B7 38. R–N2 R–Q8ch 39. K–R2 P–B8=Q 40. BxQ RxB and White resigned.*

Black's strengths became more pronounced with the queen exchange in that game. Sometimes the exchange of queens will bring only equality. But when the alternative is a bad middle-game, there is little choice.

Janowski–Tartakower, Semmering 1926
White to move

White's two bishops may have a future, but White must first do something about Black's excellently centralized queen. The simplest way of holding the two threatened White pawns (K5, QR2) is 1. B–K4. But that permits 1. . . . QxQch, and White sees that he has little after 2. KxQ KR–Q1ch 3. K–B1 N–R4 and even less after 3. K–K2 N–Q5ch 4. K–K3 BxB 5. KxB N–B4! 6. B–B2 (6. . . . R–Q5 mate was threatened) R–Q7.

1. Q–K2?

This is a clever way of holding the pawns. White directly holds the KP and indirectly prevents 1. . . . QxRP with 2. 0–0 (threat-

ening 3. Q–K4 P–N3 4. RxN). After 2. 0–0 Black must worry
about possible snares of his queen and must also avoid 2. . . .
Q–Q4 3. B–K4 Q–B4ch 4. B–B2 N–Q5 5. Q–Q1.

| 1. . . . | N–Q5 |
| 2. Q–KB2 | N–B4 |

Now Black keeps his small fire glowing. After 3. 0–0 QxRP he
at least has a solid pawn. And on 3. BxN PxB 4. P–QR3 B–R3 he
catches the White king in the center. The best is 3. P–QR3, but
after 3. . . . QR–B1 4. RxR RxR Black has a fine game and excellent winning chances.

| 3. B–K4 | QxRP! |

Black wins material (4. BxB Q–N8ch 5. K–Q2 QxPch and 6. . . .
KR–Q1ch) whatever happens. What did happen is that White
had to exchange queens (4. B–B4 BxB 5. PxB Q–N8ch 6. B–B1
QxPch 7. Q–K2), two pawns and seven moves too late.

An exchange of queens is sometimes played automatically when
a player is ahead in material. When the material difference is
great, the exchange is almost always good. But when material
is nearly in balance, it takes some hard evaluation before sweep-
ing the board of heavy pieces.

Larsen–Petrosian, Havana 1966
White to move

The material advantage to White is significant only if White
also has some positional trumps (e.g., open lines for his rooks).

But here it is Black who has most of the trumps (such as his passed QP), and it would be fair to consider the position in balance. If White wanted safety he could play 1. RxP BxR 2. QxB with a liquidation that brings the game much closer to a draw.

1. Q–K6ch?	**Q–B2**
2. QxQch	**KxQ**

The advantage of White's rooks has actually been lessened by an exchange of queens. For instance, on 3. R–K5! Black turns out to have better chances than White with 3. . . . R–QN1! 4. P–B3 (4. RxP? B–K5 followed by 5. . . . BxR or 5. . . . R–N8ch) 4. . . . R–N6 5. RxP RxP.

3. R–N2?	**P–B5**
4. P–B3	**P–Q5!**

And now the White rooks become totally passive since they can never allow the enemy pawns to advance (5. PxP P–B6). In the finale Black was too far ahead: *5. R–QB1 K–K3 6. K–B2 B–K5 7. P–B4 R–K1 8. P–N4 B–B3 9. R–K1ch K–Q4 10. RxR BxR 11. PxP P–B6 12. R–N8 P–Q7 13. R–Q8ch K–B5 14. R–B8ch K–Q6 White resigns.*

The Temporary Invasion

Under positional errors we'll consider the evils of creating pawn holes in your position. But trying to exploit such holes prematurely is a different kind of mistake and is essentially a misuse of pieces.

The occupation of a hole may seem to be dynamically aggressive, but it is often only symbolically so. You can give away many meaningless squares during a game and still prosper. But prematurely invading such a square left open by your opponent can lead to embarrassment.

Gligoric–Smyslov, Zurich 1953—*1. P–QB4 N–KB3 2. N–QB3 P–K3 3. N–B3 P–B4 4. P–KN3 P–QN3 5. B–N2 B–N2 6. 0–0 B–K2 7. P–Q4 PxP 8. QxP 0–0 9. R–Q1 N–B3 10. Q–B4 Q–N1 11. QxQ QRxQ 12. B–B4 QR–B1 13. B–Q6?!*

Position after 13. B–Q6

By occupying Q6 White keeps Black from gaining breathing space for his pieces with . . . P–Q3 or . . . P–Q4. But this otherwise painless occupation cannot be maintained for long. White actually had better winning prospects—although they weren't substantial—with 13. N–K5.

| 13. . . . | BxB! |
| 14. RxB | N–K2 |

Black gets ready to oust the outsider with 15. . . . N–B4 or 15. . . . R–B2 and 16. . . . N–B1. He also uncovers an attack on the enemy QBP, which White defends with another clumsy advance into hostile territory.

15. N–K5?	BxB
16. KxB	N–B4
17. R–Q2	P–Q3

White will not only be thrown completely back but will lose his QBP in the process. A complete fiasco, prompted by the illusion of progress by moves such as B–Q6 and N–K5.

Another version of this involving the same square:

Lewi–Witkovski, Lublin 1969—*1. P–QB4 N–KB3 2. P–KN3 P–B3 3. N–KB3 P–Q4 4. P–N3 P–K3 5. B–QN2 B–K2 6. P–Q3 QN–Q2 7. B–N2 0–0 8. 0–0 P–QN3 9. Q–B2 B–N2 10. P–K4 N–B4 11. N–B3 PxKP 12. PxP*

Position after 12. PxP

Black has a solid though cramped game. He should play something like 12. . . . Q–B2 or 12. . . . P–QR4; e.g., 12. . . . P–QR4 13. QR–Q1 Q–B2 14. P–QR3 KR–Q1 15. P–QN4 PxP 16. PxP N–R3 or 14. P–K5 KN–Q2 15. KR–K1 KR–Q1 and 16. . . . N–B1. White can quickly find himself overextended in these positions with a weak KP or QNP. Meanwhile Black would have no serious weakness.

12. . . .	**Q–Q6?**

This *looks* good since White has only one move to avoid the queen exchange that eases Black's game.

13. Q–B1!

But this, the only move, is quite playable. White threatens to win the advanced queen with 14. R–Q1. Black's only alternative to the humble (but best) 13. . . . Q–Q1 is a bad middlegame.

13. . . .	**KNxP?**
14. R–Q1	**NxN**
15. BxN!	

Perhaps Black counted on 15. RxQ N–K7ch and 16. . . . NxQ. The new position, however, favors White's bishops even if he couldn't win back a pawn. But he can: *15. . . . Q–B4* (15. . . . Q–N3 16. N–K5) *16. N–Q4 Q–N3 17. NxBP BxN* (or 17. . . . B–B3 18. P–QN4!) *18. BxB QR–B1 19. B–KN2 KR–Q1 20. Q–N2 Q–N5 21. Q–B2 Q–N3 22. QxQ RPxQ.*

Black traded queens to avoid the steady middlegame squash

that would follow P–QN4. But this same fate awaits him in the ending: 23. *K–B1 K–B1* 24. *K–K2 B–B3* 25. *BxB PxB* 26. *RxRch RxR* 27. *P–QN4! N–R3* (27. . . . N–Q6? 28. R–Q1) 28. *P–QR3 K–K2* 29. *R–QB1 R–Q2* 30. *B–K4 R–B2* 31. *P–B4 N–N1* 32. *K–K3 N–Q2* 33. *P–KR4 K–Q3* 34. *B–Q3 P–B4* 35. *K–Q4 P–B3?* 36. *P–R5! PxP* 37. *R–KR1 P–K4ch?* 38. *K–K3 P–K5* 39. *B–K2 P–R4* 40. *RxP PxP* 41. *PxP K–K3* 42. *P–N4!*, and Black resigned shortly.

Special Cases: Castling into It

The "it" you are castling into is an attack that wouldn't mean much without the presence of your king. And since castling is the one routine developing move that players rarely question, it frequently becomes a bad, if not losing move.

Many inexperienced players learn the hard way to get their king to safety early in the game. But this advice remains unqualified as they mature. It should be tempered by equally hard lessons, such as:

Pachman–Guimard, Prague 1946—1. *P–K4 P–K3* 2. *P–Q4 P–Q4* 3. *N–Q2 N–QB3* 4. *KN–B3 N–KB3* 5. *P–K5 N–Q2* 6. *P–KN3 B–K2* 7. *B–R3 P–KR4?!* 8. *0–0??*

Position after 8. 0–0

White's development makes good sense. He prepares to meet Black's . . . P–KB3 plan, since that is the only immediate method Black has of gaining counterplay. If and when Black plays . . .

P–B3, White will have a bishop bearing down on the then weak K6. White wasn't worried about 8. . . . P–R5 because after 9. B–N2 P–R6 10. B–R1 the Black KRP will inevitably fall, and after 9. . . . PxP 10. BPxP White's attack is much better than Black's because he is better developed.

8. . . .	**P–KN4**

This is the move—the winning move—White underestimated. The situation is beyond help since . . . P–N5 will either fork two pieces or (after 9. B–N2 P–N5) win the White QP. The only way of meeting . . . P–N5 is 9. *P–KN4,* but since White has castled the aeration of his kingside is terminal.

    9. . . . *PxP 10. BxP P–B4! 11. PxP e.p. NxBP 12. P–KR3 NxB 13. PxN P–K4! 14. NxP NxN 15. PxN B–K3 16. N–N3 Q–Q2 17. P–KB3 0–0–0 18. K–N2 P–Q5 19. B–Q2 Q–Q4 20. B–K1 BxP,* and White resigned shortly.

The point is clear: there is no major target in most positions until the king is castled. This is especially true of closed and semiclosed center games. When the center is blocked, there is no rush to castle because the king is naturally protected by the pawn wall immediately in front of it. When you do castle in a closed-center game it is more likely that you will be attacked than if the center were open. (Wing attacks are best met by counterattacks in the center. But if there is a blocked center, the counterattack is lessened.)

In the next game Black could castle effectively on move 7—not to bring his king to safety as much as to support 8. . . . P–B4!. He does castle two moves later when he should have decided to remain indefinitely in the center with 9. . . . P–KR4 10. Q–B4 QN–K2.

Kaplan–Timman, Jerusalem 1967—*1. P–K4 P–K3 2. P–Q4 P–Q4 3. N–QB3 B–N5 4. P–K5 P–QB4 5. Q–N4 N–K2 6. PxP QN–B3 7. B–Q2 N–B4 8. N–B3 BxP 9. B–Q3 0–0? 10. B–KN5 Q–N3 11. 0–0 Q–N5 12. Q–R3 P–KR3* (12. . . . QxP 13. N–QR4 Q–N5 14. NxB and 15. P–N4 pins and wins a piece) *13. P–R3 Q–N3 14. BxN KPxB* (14. . . . RPxB 15. Q–R7 mate) *15. NxP QxP 16. N–B6ch! PxN 17. BxBP K–R2 18. Q–R5 Black resigns.*

Castling can be delayed until the pawn center and piece development is clear enough to indicate where and how the middlegame will be fought. These factors will determine where your king belongs—not only castled or uncastled, but on which side.

Barczay–Udovcic, Zagreb 1969
Position after 8. . . . 0–0

In the diagram White has a good game since Black's pieces are stifled by his backward QP. The inability to play . . . P–Q3 is a natural consequence of the opening (*1. P–K4 P–QB4 2. N–KB3 N–KB3 3. P–K5 N–Q4 4. N–B3 NxN 5. QPxN! N–B3 6. B–QB4 P–K3 7. B–B4 B–K2 8. Q–Q2 0–0*) and influences White's decision of where to put his king. Since he wants to stop . . . P–Q3 permanently and also to keep the option of kingside attack with P–KR4 and R–R3–N3, he played:

9. 0–0–0??	**Q–R4**
10. K–N1	

Castling queenside had many good points, but a move can be terrible no matter how numerous its benefits. The main thing that 9. 0–0–0 does to the position is give Black a king to attack. He was already threatening 10. . . . P–QN4 11. B–Q3 QxRP or 11. B–QN3 P–B5.

10. . . .	**P–QN4**
11. B–Q3	**P–B5**
12. B–K4	**R–N1**

Either here or earlier White might try P–QR3 to stop . . . P–N5. But this only insures that . . . P–N5 will have greater force when it is supported by . . . P–QR4. Right now Black doesn't even need preparation—13. P–QR3 P–N5! 14. RPxP (or 14. BPxP) BxP! 15. PxB NxNP with a deadly attack.

13. N–Q4	P–N5!
14. NxN	

Neither 14. BxN PxP nor 14. PxP BxP 15. Q–K3 B–B6 could save White's king.

14. . . .	PxN
15. PxP	BxP

And White resigned, knowing that Black would drop the bishop onto R6 or B6 after he moves his queen (16. Q–B1 B–R6 or 16. P–QB3 BxP).

Wrong Rook

Another special case involves the last pieces to be positioned for the middlegame. The rooks don't seem to do much until the later portions of the contest. Yet their placement has a lot to do with planning and long-term strategy; misplacing them will, at minimum, cost time.

When there are two open files and you have two rooks, it usually doesn't take much thought to determine where your heavy pieces belong (one on each file or doubled on one file). But when you have three files, one open file and two half-open files (open only from your end), or some other situation, the choices become harder. The basic rule is to use the rooks where they can be most flexible.

Sometimes this requires considerable foresight. For example, after *1. P–K4 P–QB4 2. N–KB3 P–Q3 3. P–Q4 PxP 4. NxP N–KB3 5. N–QB3 P–QR3 6. B–K2 P–K4 7. N–N3 B–K2 8. 0–0 0–0 9. B–KN5 B–K3 10. BxN BxB 11. N–Q5 N–Q2 12. Q–Q3 R–B1 13. P–QB3 B–N4*, it's time for White to develop his rooks. The normal squares are K1 and Q1. But on K1 the KR would not be doing much—there isn't likely to be much of an attack on the White KP and not much chance of kingside attack with R–K3.

On the other hand, the best square for the QR is probably—QR1! On that square he can support P–QR4 in case Black plays . . . . P–QN4. And even if Black delays or avoids . . . P–QN4, White can get a lot of mileage out of P–QR4–5, perhaps even bringing the rook into play via QR4. In fact, in Averbakh–Petrosian, Tiflis 1959, White began with *14. QR–Q1,* and after *14. . . . K–R1 15. B–B3 P–KN3 16. N–K3 R–B3 17. KR–K1 N–B3 18. Q–K2 P–N4* he conceded the error by playing *19. R–R1.* The loss of time, however, gave Black an excellent game after *19. . . . Q–N3 20. N–Q2 P–QR4* followed by . . . KR–QB1 and . . . P–N5. (See p. 116 for White's final error.)

There is more than time to be lost from rook misplacement. Here is an instructive example of how faulty rook placement can even get you mated.

Tkachenko–Blazhko, Sumgait 1960—*1. P–Q4 N–KB3 2. P–QB4 P–KN3 3. N–QB3 B–N2 4. P–K4 P–Q3 5. P–B3 0–0 6. B–K3 P–K4 7. P–Q5 P–B3 8. Q–Q2 PxP 9. BPxP P–QR3 10. KN–K2 QN–Q2 11. N–B1 N–B4 12. N–Q3 KN–Q2 13. P–QN4 NxNch 14. BxN P–B4 15. 0–0 P–B5 16. B–KB2 P–KN4*

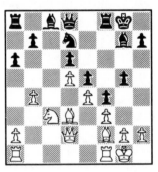

Position after 16. . . . P–KN4

The pawn structure focuses Black's attention on the kingside, White's on the queenside. White has the advantage of more space for his minor pieces and an open file for his rooks. But Black has the enemy king on the kingside. How should White continue?

1. QR–B1?	P–KR4
2. P–N5	P–N5
3. N–R4	R–B2!

Black uses his KR excellently for both defense (on the second rank in case of penetration at his QB2) and for attack (at KN2 to support . . . P–N6). Had White correctly used his KR, not QR on QB1, he could now play 4. PxP PxP 5. QR–N1 and occupy QN6 shortly. This would take some of the sting out of Black's attack. Note that White's KR is doing nothing on KB1, and it would do little more on K1 or Q1.

4. Q–N4	B–B1
5. P–N6!?	R–N2

Now Black has both . . . PxP and . . . P–N6 as line-opening threats. White's belated plan of R–QB7 won't save his king. But what would have helped was the vacancy of his KB1. If you put White's QR back on QR1 and move his KR to QB1 (as if he had played 1. KR–QB1!), White could bring his king to safety with 6. K–B1! (followed possibly by K–K2).

6. K–R1	P–N6
7. B–N1	N–B4!
8. NxN	PxN
9. RxP?!	

This desperation sacrifice is preferable to 9. BxP Q–R5 10. P–KR3 BxP but hardly good. There was no help anyway; e.g., 9. Q–N2 P–R5 10. P–KR3 BxP.

9. . . .	B–R6!
10. Q–B4	BxPch
11. KxB	PxPch
12. K–B2	BxRch
White resigns	

Calculation and Miscalculation

There's a kind of player familiar to anyone who has ever visited a European-style chess coffeehouse. In those dimly lit retreats there will always be an oldtimer who sits at a board, mug in hand, eyes glazed, muttering to himself: ". . . so he attacks me, and I attack him, and he takes me, and I take him, and then he . . ."

We all calculate like this, although we may not recognize it as calculation. Calculation sounds like something the grandmasters do when processing twenty-two-move combinations through their heads. But calculations can be and usually are much shorter—only two or three moves in length.

The opportunities for error, however, are limitless. Sometimes we make an error in the sequence of moves, counting on 1. BxP PxB 2. N–B5 when the proper course is 1. N–B5 and then 2. BxP, for example. Or we overlook a forcing move by our opponent that suddenly appears in the middle of our intended sequence and alters its consequences. Or, perhaps, we don't look far enough into the future, or misevaluate the position at the end of the sequence.

Here is a look at the basic pitfalls of calculation.

Faulty Assumption

"Never assume," Spencer Tracy, a computer expert, tells Katharine Hepburn in the 1955 movie *Desk Set*. He then poses a mystery that runs something like this: Fred and Eloise are found dead of suffocation on the floor of their apartment. Splinters of glass are found near the bodies and the carpet is wet. How did their death come about?

Katharine Hepburn muses a bit, repeats "Never assume, eh?" and reaches a deduction that would have made Sherlock Holmes proud. Fred and Eloise are goldfish who died when the bowl in which they were swimming tipped over and smashed on the floor. Without water they could not breath.

You shouldn't have assumed Fred and Eloise were humans. But chess players have to make assumptions in order to calculate. You can't progress from the first move of a combination to your second move without some supposition about what the enemy is doing in between.

Quiet moves overlooked and zwischenzugs ignored are some of the many cases of faulty assumption. Occasionally you can look pretty silly because things didn't happen the way you assumed they would.

Rubinstein–Duras, San Sebastian 1912
White to move

1. RxR

Played with the assumption that Black would recapture with his rook and accept an inferior endgame after 1. . . . RxR 2. QxQ RxQ 3. R–K7. It is a perfectly correct line of thinking with a correct evaluation. White is better after 3. R–K7 because of his superior rook; e.g., 3. . . . R–KB1 4. P–KN4 or 3. . . . NxNP 4.

NxBP BxN 5. RxB K–R1 6. R–R7 N–Q6 7. RxRP N–B4 8. R–Q6
and 9. N–Q2.

It is Black who has a shortcircuited calculation now. He decides
to interpolate 1. . . . QxQ, assuming that 2. RxRch KxR 3. PxQ
NxR with a perfectly safe minor-piece ending will follow. The
conclusion is OK but . . .

1. . . .   QxQ??
2. PxQ!

How obvious. Yet Black, a veteran grandmaster, overlooked
the simple win of a piece. He resigned after 2. . . . NxR 3. RxN!
P–R3 4. N–R3 R–B1 5. N–B4 K–R2 6. P–R5.

Endgames involve far more calculation than it is generally
thought, and this leaves plenty of room for assumption error.
For example, in one grandmaster game at the turn of the century White had a rook on QR4 and a king on KB3. Black's king
was on his KN3, his rook was at KB4, giving check, and the pawn
he hoped to win with stood at KB3. White could have drawn
using a time-honored technique of keeping his king in front of the
pawn, such as on his KB1, the pawn's queening square. Black can
advance his pawn, shepherded by his king, up to the sixth rank.
But when the pawn reaches the sixth rank, White drops his rook
to Black's side of the board and eventually gives a series of perpetual checks. Black's king can avoid the checks only by offering
a trade of rooks. He can no longer hide in front of the pawn.)
The exchange of rooks, however, leads to an elementary—and
quite drawn—endgame.

But White saw a different way of drawing. Rather than spend
several moves being pushed back, he decided to offer the trade
of rooks immediately with *1. R–KB4??*. He assumed that Black
would exchange into the simple ending (1. . . . RxRch 2. KxR
P–B4 3. K–B3 K–N4 4. K–N3 P–B5ch 5. K–B3 K–B4 6. K–B2
K–N5 7. K–N2 P–B6ch 8. K–B2 K–B5 9. K–B1! K–N6 10. K–N1!
P–B7ch 10. K–B1 K–B6 stalemate).

However, Black upset this plan with *1. . . . K–N4—the only
other playable move on the board*. White never even considered

it, but it wins just as surely as 1. . . . RxRch, the assumed move, would draw (2. RxRch KxR 3. K–N3 K–K5! 4. K–B2 K–B5! 5. K–K2 K–N6 6. K–B1 P–B4 7. K–K2 P–B5 8. K–B1 K–B6! 9. K–N1 K–K7 and . . . P–B6–7–8, touchdown).

It is possible to make a wrong assumption about any kind of move, but the usual culprit is a capture or retreat. We assume that when we are forcing the tempo of the game our opponents will play logically and defend.

Van den Berg–Rajkovic, Orebro 1966
White to move

In this sharp attacking position White probably calculated this way: "I could play 1. NPxRP en passant since he has just moved . . . P–KR4. But after 1. . . . K–R2! he would close off the kingside with one of my own pawns and begin to think about taking the initiative on the queenside (. . . Q–N3–N5), in the center (. . . P–Q4), or even on the kingside (. . . N–Q2xBP)."

Therefore, White reasons, "I will break into his castled position with a sacrifice, 1. B–K2 and 2. BxP. After 2. . . . PxB 3. QxRP he will have no effective way of meeting my threats of P–N6 or R–B3–R3. And he must take the bishop when I sacrifice it because otherwise he is just a pawn behind and facing the same danger of R–B3–R3."

With this in mind, White played:

1. B–K2	K–R2!
2. BxP?	R–KR1!

Belatedly White realizes that 2. . . . PxB was not at all forced and that he has removed from the board a pawn that will ease *Black's* kingside attack. Black now threatens 3. . . . PxB or simply 3. . . . K–N1, and 3. BxPch KxB! gives White no attack for a piece.

The game reached a swift conclusion: *3. B–B3ch K–N1 4. Q–N4 N–Q2 5. N–Q1?* (5. R–B2 BxN 6. PxB N–K4 was only slightly better) *5. . . . BxPch 6. K–B2 N–K4! 7. Q–N2 RxPch 8. B–K2 Q–R1! 9. R–R1 BxP White resigns.*

Overlooking Attack-Defense

Most calculations are by nature concentrated on forcing moves. We make a capture, our opponent recaptures. We threaten, he defends. In calculating this way we can't examine every choice at his disposal. Only the computers can do that—and they spend minutes to do it even at their incredible rate of considering variations.

When calculating out these sequences we sometimes fall into a psychological trap. We feel that we are the aggressor, the one who sets the tempo of play. But the trap is sprung when the enemy responds with what we'll call the "Attack-Defense" move. It's a move we overlook or underestimate, and it has great impact because it wrests the initiative from our hands. The opponent not only meets our threat but also makes one of his own. Our pieces, coordinated for attack, may be unprepared for the sudden role of defense.

Porges–Blackburne, Nuremburg 1896
Black to move

White reached this lost position through several errors—a greedy opening mistake, several mindless nondeveloping moves, and the exile of a knight to the side of the board *(1. P–K4 P–Q4 2. PxP N–KB3 3. P–QB4 P–B3 4. PxP? NxP 5. N–KB3 P–K4 6. P–Q3 B–KB4 7. N–R4? B–K3 8. B–K2 B–QB4 9. 0–0 Q–K2 10. P–QR3? R–Q1 11. P–QN3? 0–0 12. B–N2 P–K5 13. Q–B2? N–Q5 14. BxN BxB 15. R–R2 P–KN4 16. PxP PxN 17. K–R1 K–R1 18. N–B3 R–KN1 19. N–Q5 NxN? 20. KPxN).*

Black, who incidentally was one of the keenest tactical minds of the last century, has been forcing the tempo of play since the 10th move. He could have won smoothly with 19. . . . BxN 20. KPxB Q–K5 or 20. . . . N–K5 but preferred the following:

20. . . .   **Q–N4?**

Black threatens mate at KN7 and begins a sequence he thinks will permit him to use his extra piece for a quick win. On 21. B–B3 P–R6! 22. P–N3 Black brings his bishop to bear with 22. . . . B–KN5 or 22. . . . B–KB4.

But White has another defense to the mate threat.

21. Q–K4!

Oops. In the tactics chapter we mentioned how easy it was for the defender to overlook a double attack. Here it is the attacker who makes an oversight, and what he overlooks is the dual purpose of 21. Q–K4. It not only defends KN2 but threatens QxBch. And the forcing nature of a threat to capture a piece with check would buy time to play PxB. Since neither 21. . . . B–KB4 22. QxBch R–N2 23. R–KN1 nor 21. . . . B–QB4 22. PxB offers more than a slim chance of a draw, Black went in for one last trick:

21. . . .	**RxP!?**
22. PxR	**BxQP**
23. QxBch	**P–B3**

And now 24. P–B3 allows 24. . . . QxP mate, and 24. B–B3 BxB and 24. R–KN1 BxPch also turn the game around again. But . . .

24. B–N4!

Black had to resign after 24. . . . B–B3 25. P–B3 or play out this dismal position a full rook down.

In a more positional vein we find White led astray below by overoptimism and another Attack-Defense move.

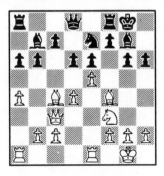

Barczay–Ivkov, Sousse 1967
White to move

Part of the blame for what happens can be laid to White's evaluation of the opening *(1. P–K4 P–KN3 2. P–Q4 B–N2 3. N–KB3 P–Q3 4. B–QB4 P–QR3!? 5. 0–0 P–K3!? 6. B–KN5 N–K2 7. Q–Q2 P–R3 8. B–K3 N–Q2 9. N–B3 P–N3 10. KR–K1 B–N2 11. P–QR4 N–KB3! 12. P–K5 N(3)–Q4 13. B–B4 NxN 14. QxN 0–0).* White looks for a way of punishing his opponent's extravagant play. But there is actually nothing wrong with Black's present position. The time for punishment is past.

Instead of opting for a modest advantage in space with 15. Q–N3 or 15. Q–Q2, hoping to provoke Black into restricting his own pieces with 15. ... P–Q4?, White calculates a forcing line with 15. PxP (a capture) PxP 16. Q–R3 (a threat). He tries to use his threat to capture the Black QP as a way of provoking it to advance.

15. PxP?!	**PxP**
16. Q–R3?	**N–B4!**

It's time for White to see that 16. ... N–B4 not only defends but threatens (17. ... BxN 18. QxB NxP). White didn't see enough though. He saves his QP at a much greater cost to his position.

17. P–B3?	**BxN!**
18. PxB	**P–K4**

Here, after 19. PxP PxP 20. BxKP, Black would have his choice between winning the Exchange (20. . . . BxB 21. RxB Q–N4ch 22. K–moves N–N6ch) or playing for mate (20. . . . N–R5). White's pieces are disastrously tangled on the kingside because of his miscalculation at move 16. What happens next is no surprise.

19. B–KN3	**P–KR4!**
20. PxP	**PxP**
21. K–R1	**Q–N4**

White resigned here since 22. R–KN1 P–R5 23. BxKP Q–R4! would win a piece with the double attack on bishop and king (24. BxB QxPch 25. R–N2 P–R6).

It must also be noted that a good Attack-Defense move can be met by an equally good Attack-Defense move.

Korchnoi–Fischer, Curacao 1962
White to move

White clearly has all the big chips. He has an extra pawn and controls the open queenside lines, so he will be able to make use of that pawn in the middlegame. There are many consolidating moves that suggest themselves, but White overfinessed.

1. B–B6

The threat of P–N5–N6–N7 forces Black to take the bishop. White had probably concluded that 1. . . . NxB 2. R–QB1 Q–N3 3. PxN QxNP 4. Q–Q5 would end the game quickly. Even with material equality Black would be lost trying to stop a dangerous passed pawn and meet numerous kingside dangers. Or so it seemed.

1. ...	NxB
2. R–QB1	Q–R2!

This trick, meeting the threat of capturing the knight with an attack on the rival queen, is probably what White overlooked when he calculated 1. B–B6.

I say "probably" because White may have foreseen this position and assumed he would win the piece back with an Attack-Defense move of his own, a queen check that defends against 3. ... QxQ but also attacks the enemy king.

3. Q–N2ch	QN–K4!

But this response ends the forcing sequence in Black's favor. It is another move with two purposes—stopping check and saving a knight—and leaves Black permanently a piece ahead.

Overlooked Zwischenzug

The German language has given us some glorious words for chess mistakes, including *wopatzerschach* and *harikarizug* (a move that commits Oriental-style suicide). It has also left us *zwischenzug* or in-between move, the uninvited guest that steps into your calculations and pushes everybody out of the way. A zwischenzug can cause chaos because it is more forceful—being usually a check, threat of mate, or attack on a valuable piece—than the other moves in the intended sequence. Not all such violent interpolations are good. But they must be considered.

Steinitz–Anderssen, Vienna 1873
Black to move

This position is strikingly modern although it occurred more than a century ago between the two best players of the day. (It derived from *1. P–Q4 P–Q4 2. P–QB4 P–K3 3. N–QB3 N–KB3 4. B–N5 B–K2 5. P–K3 0–0 6. N–B3 P–QN3 7. B–Q3 B–N2 8. 0–0 QN–Q2 9. PxP PxP 10. R–B1 P–B4 11. PxP PxP 12. Q–R4.*)

Black's position is under some pressure because of the vulnerability of his two central "hanging" pawns. The best way of defending the pawns is for Black to coordinate his heavy pieces with 12. . . . Q–N3 followed by . . . KR–Q1 and . . . QR–B1. But he chose another way of liquidating pressure and set off a torrent of zwischenzug possibilities which ultimately backfired.

12. . . .   **N–K5?**

The knight move is based on calculations involving the White bishop on KN5. If that bishop were on KB4 White would now pocket a pawn with 13. NxN. But as the pieces stand, Black is OK after 13. NxN PxN 14. BxP because of 14. . . . QBxB!. In this variation White would lose a piece after 15. BxB QxB because the Black bishop on K5 is suddenly protected. White could recoup his material with 15. QxB BxB and now the zwischenzug 16. KR–Q1. But even then Black would have accomplished what he had set out to do: relieve pressure (16. . . . B–B3 17. Q–B5 Q–R4 18. RxN QxP).

After 12. . . . N–K5 there is a trio of zwischenzug traps for Black to fall into. After 13. NxN PxN 14. BxP he could try for a winning advantage with 14. . . . N–N3!?, removing a piece from danger and attacking the White queen (15. QBxB QxB or 15. Q–B2 QBxB 16. QxB BxB 17. KR–Q1 Q–K2 with an extra piece). However, 14. . . . N–N3 is a blunder because of the *counterzwischenzug* 15. BxPch! (15. . . . KxB 16. Q–R4ch K–N1 17. BxB or 15. . . . K–R1 16. Q–R4).

The other two traps also involve counterzwischenzugs: *(a)* 12. . . . N–K5 13. NxN N–N3? (hoping for 14. BxB QxB 15. Q–B2 PxN or 15. Q–B2 PxN) 14. N–B6ch! BxB 15. Q–R4 P–R3 16. BxB, and *(b)* 12. . . . N–K5 13. BxB NxN? 14. Q–R4!. What an unusually rich collection of captures and threats!

13. BxN!   PxB

Clearly Black cannot take the other bishop (13. . . . BxB 14. BxQP). He had probably calculated 12. . . . N–K5 13. BxN PxB 14. BxB QxB 15. N–Q2 and come to the conclusion that Black's position was acceptable after 15. . . . N–B3 because the weakness of his QBP is offset by White's weaknesses on the kingside and at his Q3.

Position after 13. . . . PxB

14. KR–Q1!

This is the shot Black overlooked or underestimated. White will meet 14. . . . PxB or 14. . . . BxB with 15. RxN, which gains time for a second capture by attacking the Black queen. Black may have seen this far but assumed that 14. KR–Q1 could be handled by 14. . . . BxB 15. RxN Q–B1! threatening 16. . . . B–QB3 as well as 16. . . . PxN and 16. . . . B–KB3.

14. . . .	BxB
15. NxB!	QxN
16. RxN	

Both sides have run out of things to capture, and we can now appreciate White's superiority. He will win at least one of the many weak pawns (e.g., 16. . . . B–B1 17. R–B7 B–R6 18. QxKP or simply 17. R–Q5!; 16. . . . QR–N1 QxRP).

White finished off with a fine example of tactical winning technique: *16. . . . KR–N1 17. Q–N3!* (a double attack and much better than 17. NxP Q–N3 when it is Black who has twin threats of 18. . . . QxN and 18. . . . B–B3) *17. . . . B–B3 18. QxPch K–R1 19. P–KR4! Q–N5 20. RxP RxR 21. QxR RxP 22. QxP Q–K3 23. R–Q1* (first-rank threat) *P–R3 24. R–Q6* (fork) *Q–B2 25. N–Q1!* (attack—of the rook—and defense—of KB2) *R–K7 26. K–B1! Black resigns*. Something must fall.

In this last example Black lost because he didn't count on his opponent's zwischenzug. But failing to find your own interpolations can be just as costly.

Belyavsky–Stean, Moscow 1975
White to move

This is the kind of critical moment that frequently occurs when a sacrificial attack has failed to smash an opponent. White has enough material for his sacrificed rook—two minor pieces and two pawns—but he appears to be losing the initiative to a powerful Black counterattack. Instead of consolidating his position and preparing for defense, he looked for a brilliant way of continuing the attack. It's all very clever and consistent. And bad.

1. RxP!??

The cleverness lies in 1. . . . QxR 2. QxBch followed by B–R5(ch) and 1. . . . KxR 2. R–B1ch K–K3 3. QxN, in both cases with new life for the attack. The new sacrifice is sufficiently forcing (1. . . . BxQ 2. RxQ or 1. . . . Q–Q3 2. RxNch QxR 3. QxBch), so Black looks for a zwischenzug.

1. . . .	BxPch
2. K–R1	QxR

With the aid of the in-between . . . BxPch/K–R1, Black can take the rook under what seems to be safer circumstances than 1. . . . QxR 2. QxB.

3. R–KB1!

But this ruptures Black's defense. He cannot permit 4. B–R5ch or 4. RxNch but must do something with his queen. The best try is to sacrifice it, but in the ensuing position it only takes a few slight inaccuracies to end the game: 3. . . . *QxRch 4. BxQ B–Q3 5. Q–Q4 K–Q2 6. B–K2 R–N1?* (6. . . . K–B2) 7. *B–N4ch N–K3?* (7. . . . K–B2 8. BxB RxB 9. Q–R4 loses a valuable RP but is better than this) 8. *Q–B6! Black resigns.*

After the game the loser noted that when "there is one and only one playable variation; there is no excuse for not seeing it." Of course, you have to know that such a variation exists to make such a search. But had Black looked hard enough he would have found a saving—and perhaps winning—line: 1. . . . KxR 2. R–B1ch B–B4!!.

This other zwischenzug returns a piece while gaining valuable time after 3. RxBch K–K3. With his first rank clear and a knight protecting the rook, White's two main attacking pieces are in danger. There are a number of escape tries (3. B–R5ch K–K2; 3. B–B4ch K–K2), but the best chance is 3. RxBch K–K3 4. Q–N8ch! KxR 5. Q–N4ch K–B3 6. Q–B3ch K–N2 7. QxR even though 7. . . . BxPch 8. K–B1 P–QR4! favors Black.

Finally, zwischenzugs play an important role positionally as well as tactically. A slight interpolation may not mean much in material won or mates threatened, but it can do wonders for the overall strategic chances.

Bronstein–Aronin, Moscow 1955
Black to move

Here Black has defended rather riskily in the center and faces a readymade kingside attack. (The game began *1. P–K4 P–QB4 2. N–KB3 N–QB3 3. B–N5 Q–B2 4. 0–0 P–K3 5. P–B3 N–B3 6. Q–K2 P–Q4 7. P–K5 N–Q2 8. P–Q4 B–K2 9. PxP NxBP 10. P–QN4 N–K5?! 11. N–Q4! P–KR3 12. P–B3 N–N4 13. B–K3 0–0 14. N–Q2 P–B4 15. P–KB4 N–K5 16. QNxN.*)

Suppose Black recaptures on K5 with his QP. White would then have good prospects on the queenside with 17. NxN! PxN 18. B–B4 followed by Q–KB2, KR–Q1, B–B5xB, and Q–B5 or R–Q6 to exploit Black's weak Q3 square and isolated QBP. Black could anticipate all this with 18. . . . P–B4, but then 19. P–N5! followed by P–QR4, Q–R2, KR–N1, and P–R5 gives White another good plan.

Black could also recapture on K5 with his BP, although this exposes his KP and kingside to danger after 17. BxN PxB 18. Q–N4. Still, this is the best chance since the pawn on Black's K5 interferes with much of White's kingside play by preventing R–KB3–R3 and closing off the QN1–KR7 diagonal.

Nevertheless, Black played a logical zwischenzug:

16. . . .   NxN

This interpolation enables him to recapture on K5 next move without worrying about a capture on his own QB3.

17. N–B6ch!

But this counterzwischenzug upsets the balance. It keeps a Black pawn off K5, thereby aiding a White attack, and it gains a tempo for that attack after 17. . . . BxN or 17. . . . RxN because Black would have to retreat a piece on his 18th move (17. . . . PxN?? 18. BxN would insure the opening of the center and king-side and is even worse for Black than what happens).

What happened was *17. . . . RxN 18. BxN R–B1 19. P–N4! B–Q2 20. B–Q3! P–KN3* (20. . . . PxP 21. QxP and 22. Q–N6) *21. K–R1 K–R2 22. R–KN1 P–R3 23. P–QR4 R–KN1 24. R–N3 QR–KB1 25. R–KR3 B–K1 26. R–KN1?* (26. P–R5!) *BxP 27. PxP KPxP 28. Q–N2 B–K1 29. RxPch? KxR 30. Q–R3ch K–N2 31. P–K6ch B–B3??* (31. . . . R–B3 32. QxP? K–B1 wins for Black) *32. QxP! BxB 33. RxPch BxR 34. QxBch Black resigns* (34. . . . K–R1 35. Q–R6ch). Despite the mutual errors after 17. N–B6ch, White's victory was a natural result.

Overlooking a Quiet Move

Of all the moves to overlook when calculating, the most sur-prising is the quiet response in a position when "loud" moves are expected. Instead of a check, a capture, or a threat in a position rife with possibilities, we are faced with a nonviolent answer. Such quiet moves often are just bad moves, accomplishing noth-ing. But sometimes they are the perfectly unsettling response.

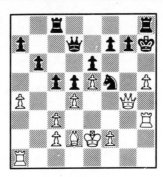

Mazzoni–O'Kelly, Paris 1963
White to move

Black is briskly attacking on the queenside (1. K–Q3 PxP 2. PxP R–B5) and staunchly defending on the kingside (1. P–R6 P–N3!) here. Appreciating this, White went into a deep huddle. He considered doubling rooks along the KN-file with 1. R–KN1 and 2. R(3)–N3. That would threaten 3. QxPch! NxQ 4. RxN mate. Black, of course, could play 2. . . . NxRch, eliminating one of the attackers. But after 3. RxN Black would have lost one of his defenders of KN2 as well. Clearly, Black could not afford to defend that point with 3. . . . . P–N3. So, White reasoned, Black would have to cover the square with a rook.

All this seems to leave Black safe, but White's calculations uncovered a brilliant resource. Whether Black takes the Exchange with . . . NxRch or not, once he puts a rook at KN1 White will have the brilliant Q–N6ch!!. After . . . PxQ, White plays PxPch and then checks along the KR-file. The only flight square, KN1, has now been occupied by a Black rook and it is mate, White thought. Q.E.D. So . . .

1. R–KN1?!	PxP
2. R(3)–N3	KR–N1
3. Q–N6ch??	K–R1!

White assumed that Black would know enough to take a queen when offered one. But this assumption is the big hole in his combination. He may have been victimized also by a visual error—failing to see that Black's KR1 would become vacant—when he began his long think at the previous diagram.

In any event, *everything* is hanging thanks to Black's delight-fully quiet response. He threatens to win pawns and an Exchange. But most of all he threatens 4. . . . PxQ (5. PxP NxRch 6. RxN KR–Q1 7. R–R3ch K–N1). White's doom was sealed, and Black took his time to guarantee victory: *4. Q–N5 Q–Q1 5. Q–N4 (5. QxQ permits the zwischenzug 5. . . . NxRch) Q–B2 6. P–R6 (6. PxP Q–B5ch is another speedy loss) QxPch 7. K–Q1 NxR 8. RxN NPxP 9. Q–R4 RxR 10. PxR Q–B4 11. QxRPch K–N1 12. PxP QxPch 13. K–K1 Q–N3 14. Q–B4 Q–K5ch White resigns.*

Only in the most docile positions can you guess with total assurance of what your opponent will do. Yet even in such a situation, there is room for self-deception.

Najdorf–Opocensky, Prague 1946
Black to move

In this example Black is victimized by several kinds of errors. First, he sees himself reduced to passivity, with his king and rook tied in the defense of his KBP (1. . . . K–B3?? 2. N–Q7ch). He thinks he needs an active defense to hold the draw.

Had he asked "How can I lose?" he would have realized that the only ways would be *(a)* the penetration of the White king to a Black target, *(b)* being reduced to zugzwang, or *(c)* the crea-tion of a decisive White breakthrough with P–KB5. But pene-tration is impossible, the pawn break on KB5 is not enough to win for White, and the attempt at zugzwang should not work after, say, 1. . . . N–B3 2. K–B2 N–R2 3. K–K3 N–B3 4. K–B4

N–R2 5. P–N4 PxP 6. PxP N–B3 7. P–N5 N–R4ch 8. K–N4 K–N1 since Black can play . . . K–N1–N2 forever.

The final contributing error is Black's failure to see a quiet move:

1. . . .   **P–N4??**

Black figures that 2. PxP NxP will stop White's idea of P–KN4–5 and will also keep the White king at bay since 3. K–R3 is illegal.

2. K–R3!

But Black didn't consider this quiet response to the "loud" 1. . . . P–N4. Now the White king reaches KR4 and wins the KRP, after which P–KN4–5 will be a decisive plan. The end came shortly: *2. . . . K–N1 3. PxP NxPch 4. K–R4 N–R2 5. KxP K–N2 6. P–N4! N–B3ch 7. K–R4 K–N1 8. P–N5 N–R2 9. N–N4 K–N2,* and after adjournment Black resigned in face of 10. K–R5 R–KR1 11. N–R6!; e.g., 11. . . . R–KB1 12. P–K5 (zugzwang) or 11. . . . NxP 12. KxN RxN 13. RxPch (removal of defender).

Desperado

The Wild West gives us a name for this easily overlooked device.

Schlechter–Spielmann, San Sebastian 1912
White to move

Black has an isolated QP which in some games proves to be a liability. Here it gives Black a fine position in the center. Seeing this, White tries to complicate with a small sequence he hopes will expose the QP to danger.

1. Q–R5?   N–B3

White had seen this natural response, a move that both defends (KR2) and attacks. But he had counted on:

2. N–K4?

Now on 2. . . . NxN 3. BxN White has traded off a principal defender of Black's QP and kingside by using the pin along the fifth rank (3. . . . PxB??? 4. QxQ). The exchange also emphasizes the superiority of White's bishop over Black's. Meanwhile, if Black prefers 2. . . . NxQ 3. NxQ, White has a slight edge in the ending where isolated center pawns may be vulnerable targets. What White didn't consider was:

2. . . .   QxPch!

Responding to an opponent's threatening move with your own threatening move is a mistake when the enemy has a more forceful reply. Here White must capture the queen and remain a pawn behind. (In the game White was so unnerved that he blundered again a few moves later—3. *KxQ NxQ* 4. *N–N5 P–KR3* 5. *N–B3 N–B5* 6. *N–Q4 KR–K1* 7. *K–B3 P–KN4* 8. *R–K5?? NxB*, and White resigned in view of 9. PxN B–N5ch 10. PxB RxR.)

This is a form of Desperado, an appropriately named burst of violence from unsuspected quarters. It usually involves a forced sequence in which each player has an attacked piece. Since your piece is subject to imminent capture, you grab some material for it. If your opponent then captures your doomed piece, you take his and you've gained some material, as Black did with 2. . . . QxPch! above. Or he can use his doomed piece to capture some material of yours. "And he takes me, and I take him, and he takes me . . ."

Falling into a Desperado can turn even the quietest position into a miniature slaughter, as the following illustrates (it began 1. *N–KB3 N–KB3* 2. *P–Q4 P–K3* 3. *P–B4 P–QN3* 4. *P–KN3 B–N2*

5. *B–N2 B–N5ch* 6. *B–Q2 BxBch* 7. *QNxB P–Q3* 8. *0–0 0–0* 9. *R–K1 QN–Q2* 10. *Q–B2*).

Euwe–Colle, Karlsbad 1929
Black to move

10. . . .   P–K4?

Black was not calculating when he played this. He was simply making what he deemed to be a sound positional move. He wants to fix White's center pawns on white squares so that the presence of white-square bishops will benefit Black. But it is faulty because of tactics.

11. NxP!   **BxB**
12. NxN

Black had always assumed that when White moved his KN from KB3 he could play . . . BxB and force the response KxB. But White's "desperate" KN has gone down in true Desperado fashion, eating a pawn along the way. After 11. . . . PxN 12. BxB R–N1 Black might have been able to save that pawn if White had continued 13. B–N2 PxP. But White could have then inserted a different sequence, 13. PxP! RxB 14. PxN, to keep his booty. And if Black had played 11. . . . NxN 12. BxB R–N1, he would have lost a full piece by way of 13. PxN!

Black's best idea now is to cut his losses with 12. . . . QxN 13. KxB, but he permits the Desperado knight to wreak more havoc:

12. . . .   **B–R6??**
13. NxR   **Resigns**

Even when you realize that you're entering a Desperado derby, it takes a clear head to make sure that you can match your captures with your opponent's at each point in the sequence. For example, in the following game Black suddenly finds he can't match White's 16. B–K2 with 16. . . . B–K2 17. RxP RxP because of 18. RxR.

Tartakower–Rosselli del Turco, Semmering 1926—*1. P–Q4 P–Q4 2. P–QB4 P–QB3 3. N–KB3 N–B3 4. P–K3 P–K3 5. QN–Q2 QN–Q2 6. B–Q3 B–Q3 7. 0–0 0–0 8. P–K4 P–K4? 9. KPxP BPxP 10. BPxP PxP 11. N–K4! N–K4 12. B–KN5 B–KN5 13. BxN BxN 14. BxQ BxQ 15. QRxB QRxB 16. B–K2! B–N1 17. RxP N–B3 18. R(4)–Q1,* and White won the endgame.

A Desperado need not win material. It frequently does because the player who is running second in the race to capture may be tripped up by the complications. Yet there is also a danger of permitting a Desperado that scores positional points.

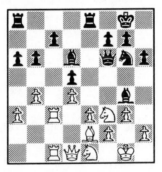

Smejkal–Langeweg, Wijk aan Zee 1975
Black to move

Here Black has an uninspiring but solid position. White can't do much immediate damage either since his massed strength on the QB–file is blunted by the protection of the Black bishop on Q3. So, assuming there was no tactical danger—that is, nothing to calculate—Black made sure his only undefended piece got some protection.

    1. . . .   **Q–B4?**
    2. N–R4!!

Black must have known his queen could be attacked in this manner. But earlier he had dismissed N–KR4 because of . . . NxN, crippling the White kingside. Now, however, White has a Desperado working. Black can't play 2. . . . NxN 3. BxB Q–N4 without losing a full piece (4. PxN QxP 5. P–R3 and 6. N–N2). Perhaps he was counting on 2. . . . BxB 3. QxB NxN.

2. . . .	**BxB**
3. NxQ!	**BxQ**
4. NxB	

Each White capture makes new threats (4. . . . B–R4? 5. NxR), and Black must ride the Desperado out until the forcing sequence ends.

4. . . .	**PxN**
5. RxB	

Now no more captures are likely, and as the dust clears, White's advantage becomes evident. His rooks will dominate the only open file, and when Black exchanges rooks, White will exploit the weak enemy pawns. This is precisely what happened.

5. . . . R(K)–QB1 6. R(1)–B1 N–K2 7. R–B7 K–B1 8. N–Q3 K–K1 9. N–B4 K–Q1 10. RxRch RxR 11. RxRch KxR 12. N–R5! P–N3 13. N–B6 P–QN4 14. K–B1 K–B2 15. P–N4 K–B3 16. P–KR4 K–N3 17. K–K1 P–QR4 18. K–Q1 PxP 19. PxP K–B3 20. K–K2 K–B2 21. K–B3 K–B3 22. P–R5! PxP 23. PxP K–B2 24. K–B4 K–B3 25. N–N4 N–N1 26. NxP!, and Black resigned in face of a lost king-and-pawn ending: 26. . . . NxN 27. K–N5 N–N1 28. P–R6 NxP 29. KxN K–Q2 30. K–N7 K–K3 31. P–B4 K–K2 32. P–B5!.

One Move Short

There comes a time when your calculated sequence must end. You look two moves ahead and conclude that you will win a piece. So you stop looking. That should send up danger signals all over: is there more life in the position after two moves—that is, more forcing play? Does he have a surprise move, a check, a capture, or an overpowering threat that turns around your evaluation of the sequence? Did you stop calculating too early?

Taimanov–Aronin, Moscow 1951
Black to move

This Sicilian Defense position contains some danger for Black. His opponent has maneuvered a bishop around to strike at the Black QP *(1. P–K4 P–QB4 2. N–KB3 P–Q3 3. P–Q4 PxP 4. NxP N–KB3 5. N–QB3 N–B3 6. B–KN5 P–K3 7. Q–Q2 P–QR3 8. 0–0–0 P–R3 9. B–KB4 B–Q2 10. B–N3)*. When White moves his knight from Q4 the QP will be exposed. Neither 10. . . . P–K4, creating a bad hole at Q4, nor 10. . . . N–K4, inviting P–KB4–5, is palatable defense of the QP.

But Black determines that there is no immediate threat to the pawn since 11. NxN BxN 12. BxP BxB 13. QxB QxQ 14. RxQ could be met by 14. . . . BxP (but not 14. . . . NxP?? 15. RxB removing the defender). So Black prepares threats against the White center pawns (. . . P–QN4–5).

10. . . .	P–QN4?
11. NxN	BxN
12. BxQP	BxB
13. QxB	QxQ
14. RxQ	BxP
15. NxB!	NxN

What is this? Is Black, who forks a rook and the KBP, all of a sudden winning? Black may have thought so. His calculations stopped here, and he looked no further when he played 10. . . . P–QN4.

16. RxRP!

No, Black's position is in ruins (16. . . . RxR 17. BxPch K–K2 18. BxR NxP 19. R–K1 or 16. . . . 0–0 17. BxP). White will not only have an extra pawn but will enjoy three connected passed pawns.

Before 16. RxRP the position seemed very calm, and Black may be forgiven for failing to look that one move more. But in a live position, one with tactical ideas all over the place, there is no excuse for not hunting down the surprise that will turn your combination to pipesmoke.

In the next example Black surely looked for surprises three moves after 21. . . . PxN. He may be excused because 24. B–N6 is a truly spectacular shot. (The game began *1. P–Q4 N–KB3 2. P–QB4 P–KN3 3. N–QB3 B–N2 4. P–K4 P–Q3 5. P–B3 0–0 6. B–K3 P–K4 7. P–Q5 N–K1 8. Q–Q2 P–KB4 9. 0–0–0 P–B5 10. B–B2 N–Q2 11. KN–K2 N–N3?! 12. Q–Q3 P–N4 13. K–N1 B–Q2 14. N–B1 P–B4? 15. PxP e.p. PxP 16. P–B5! N–B1 17. PxP KNxP 18. B–B5 R–B3 19. B–K2 Q–B2 20. N–N3 B–K1.)*

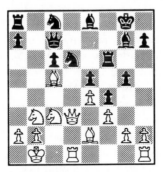

Tal–Visockiss, Leningrad 1954
White to move

Black has permitted an interesting combination beginning with 21. N–Q5. He believes it is a clever trap (21. . . . PxN 22. QxPch N–B2 23. QxR B–B3!) that will swallow up the White queen. After he had calculated as far as 23. . . . B–B3, he probably searched for a shot from White. But where is it?

White's pieces seem active enough but they need the help of

the queen to dance. So Black stopped at 23. . . . B–B3 and thought
he was safe.

21. N–Q5!	PxN
22. QxPch	N–B2
23. QxR	B–B3
24. B–N6!!	

Safe no longer. On 24. . . . QxB White escapes with his booty
by 25. QxNch. The Black queen has no safe move so Black has
to play 24. . . . PxB. But after 25. R–QB1 White saves his queen
and actually has a winning ending because of his superior minor
pieces. The game went *25. R–QB1 BxQ 26. RxQ R–B3 27.
KR–QB1 RxR 28. RxR QN–Q3 29. N–Q2 B–B1 30. B–B4 P–N4
31. B–K6 K–N2 32. P–QR4!*, and White eventually won (32. . . .
PxP 33. N–B4!).

Misjudging the Bottom Line

Even if Black had foreseen everything above, including 24.
B–N6, he might still have permitted 21. N–Q5 because he mis-
evaluated the position after 26. RxQ. It's possible he thought that
he was better in the endgame since two minor pieces are often
far superior to a rook and pawn. His calculation was OK; his
evaluation of the final position was wrong.

This is another common problem, even for computers. Like
humans, the machines have a sense of what constitutes a winning
position. They have to calculate several side variations in a
combination, and they stop considering them once they conclude
that the quiet after the storm is a good quiet.

Tchigorin–Walbrodt, Nuremberg 1896
White to move

The grandmaster who held the White pieces here was quite a fine calculator. But he went astray the way many lesser players do. He got far enough into his calculations to determine that he was winning. After all, he might have said to himself, after 5. Q–N5ch and 6. RxQ, I've won his queen.

1. N–B6!?

This is a clever way of using the White bishops and rooks before one of them is silenced by 1. . . . P–B5. But 1. N–N6 is actually much better (1. . . . Q–B2 2. BxB PxB 3. B–R5 with a positional advantage because of the weak KP).

1. . . .	PxN
2. BxPch	NxB
3. QxNch	K–N1
4. R–K5??	

This is the only way of continuing the attack for a win. At first 4. RxB(K) looks good (4. . . . PxR 5. BxPch). But then it looks bad because of 4. . . . BxPch 5. KxR QxR. And finally it looks OK since after 5. . . . QxR White can draw with 6. Q–N5ch K–R1 7. Q–B6ch. But only draw.

4. . . .	BxR
5. Q–N5ch	B–N2
6. RxQ	RxR

Now let's count up. White has won a queen. But Black has two rooks and a bishop for it—a gross imbalance. The only danger to Black now is overconfidence.

Within a dozen moves the weight of Black's material crushed White: *27. P–B3 BxB 28. PxB P–B4 29. Q–K3 R–Q8ch 30. K–B2 P–KB5 31. Q–K4 R–Q7ch 32. K–N1 RxQNP 33. P–KR4 K–R1 34. Q–Q5 BxP 35. QxBP B–N2 36. P–QN4 R–KN1 37. K–R1 RxKNP! 38. P–R5 R–Q7 39. P–R6 R–Q8ch* (White's last traps were *39. . . . BxP 40. Q–B3ch* and *39. . . . B–Q5 40. Q–K5ch!!* forcing stalemate) *40. K–R2 BxP 41. Q–K5ch B–N2 42. QxBP R–K8 43. Q–Q2 R–K3 and White resigned.*

Mistaken Sequence

Finally, there are mistakes to be made with the order of moves. You may see all the tactical ideas in a combinational position, but if you don't get them in the right order, the combination falls flat.

Tartakower–Yates, Karlsbad 1929
White to move

Forceful play has weakened Black's kingside and given White excellent centralized piece play as compensation for the Exchange. But if the attack stalls, Black stands better. Therefore, White looks for the knockout punch.

If there is one here it is sure to involve some of White's trumps: his bishop's attack on KB7, his knight's ability to check on KR6, and his queen's range. One can imagine N–R6ch, BxPch, and, after . . . K–B1, Q–R8ch or Q–B6 as the tactical components of the knockout.

1. N–R6ch?	**K–R2!**
2. NxP	

But after

2. . . .	**Q–B4!**

White must sue for peace and play 3. N–N5ch K–R3 4. N–B7ch K–R2 5. N–N5ch. Once White's queen is exchanged off or retreats from Q4, Black can play to win.

However, there was a win for White in the diagram: 1. BxPch! (1. . . . QxB 2. N–R6ch; 1. . . . KxB 2. N–R6ch K–K3 3. P–B5ch or 2. . . . K–B1 3. Q–R8ch). These same tactical tools that made up the faulty 1. N–R6ch? would have won for White if used in the correct sequence.

Reordering the sequence is one of the most easily omitted aids in calculation. In this instance, White's order of moves wasn't sufficiently forcing. There was no decisive followup after 2. . . . Q–B4. But sometimes a sequence can be too forcing. A different order of moves would leave the enemy helpless, but the one chosen gives him counterchances.

Zita–Golombek, Prague 1946
White to move

White has sacrificed a pawn to mount an attack on the king-side, specifically at KN7. Black just has enough time to cover that square and the other vital one at KB3. He is preparing to relieve the pressure and protect his KN2 with . . . P–N3!. White, therefore, looks for a method of exploiting the moment. He can't force Black's KB away, but he can do something about the queen.

1. N–B6?   Q–B2!

The flaw in White's combination was his failure to see 2. QxN QxR!, which removes his queen's defender. The idea of driving off the queen and capturing on KB6 was a good one, but once again the idea was improperly presented. With 1. B–N5! Black would have been quite lost (1. . . . K–R1 2. BxN PxB and now 3. N–B6!; or 1. . . . K–R1 2. BxN QxB 3. QxQ PxQ 4. NxP mate).

The new position on the board presents a second crisis for White. He could retreat the attacked knight to K5 or look for a consistent followup to his attack. White's last move, as faulty as it is, creates new tactical possibilities involving R–K5 and R(K)–KN5 or BxP. But again there is a good order of ideas and a bad one.

2. R–K5?

Though this threatens both 3. BxP BxB 4. R(K)–N5 and 3. QxN (now that Black can't take the rook on KN6 with his queen), it is far inferior to the right order: 2. BxP! BxB 3. R–K5 K–B1! 4. R(K)–N5 with chances.

2. . . .   P–N3!

Now we see that 2. R–K5 wasn't forceful enough. The attack on KN7 is all over, and Black's counterattack soon proved decisive: *3. BxB RxB 4. QxN QxN 5. P–R4 KR–Q1 6. R–K1 R–Q4! 7. R–KB3 Q–Q2 8. P–N3 R–QB1.*

Positional Errors

Often a player will explain his choice between two lines of play with: "I decided to make the game tactical because I was getting a bad game positionally," or "I wanted to play that move but it just looked too antipositional," or "Tactically this was a good idea, but I was afraid that it would compromise my position." These common post-mortem comments suggest there are two separate kinds of moves, positional and tactical.

In fact, the distinction is much more subtle. A good game in positional terms will create its own tactical ideas. A poor game positionally may have some short-term tactical benefits but won't be able to generate the vital threats that are needed to win in the long run against a worthy opponent.

A few years ago I won a pleasing game, which was then published in a number of chess magazines. What surprised me was the reaction of friends who played it over. They saw the queen sacrifice that ended the game and congratulated me for outplaying my opponent tactically. In truth, there was only one tactical phase of the game, the very last move.

Stoyko–Soltis, National Chess League 1977—*1. P–QB4 N–KB3 2. N–QB3 P–KN3 3. P–K4 P–Q3 4. P–Q4 B–N2 5. B–K2 0–0 6. N–B3 P–B3 7. 0–0 P–QR3 8. P–QR4 P–QR4 9. P–R3 P–K4 10. B–K3 QN–Q2 11. Q–Q2 Q–K2 12. P–Q5 N–K1 13. N–K1 P–QB4 14. P–KN4 P–B4 15. P–B3 P–R4 16. B–N5 N(2)–B3 17. KPxP NPxP 18. PxRP Q–KB2 19. P–R6 B–R1 20. P–B4 N–R4 21. BxN*

QxB 22. Q–N2 K–R2 23. N–N5 R–KN1 24. K–R1 B–Q2 25. R–R3 BxN 26. RPxB N–B3 27. Q–QB2 N–K5 28. N–N2 QR–KB1 29. P–R4 NxB 30. PxN RxP 31. RxRP R(1)–KN1 32. R–KN1 P–K5 33. R–R7 QxPch White forfeited on time.

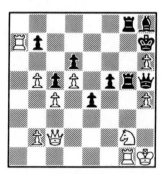

Position after 33. R–R7

After 34. NxQ RxRch 35. K–R2 B–K4ch Black mates in two more moves. It *is* a pretty finish. But the game had been decided from a positional point of view by move 18 because of White's repeated positional concessions. Let's look at the critical errors.

8 P–QR4: White sought to stop 8. . . . P–QN4 followed by 9. . . . PxP, a flanking thrust that would have given Black a majority of pawns in the center. But after 8. P–QR4? P–QR4! Black had tricked his opponent into creating a hole at White's QN4. White then had no pawns that control this square and this was a significant concession. Why? Because the nature of the center pawn structure often requires White to drum up queenside play with P–QN4–5 or P–QN4 and P–QB5. After 8. P–QR4? P–QR4! Black can meet a subsequent P–QN4 with . . . RPxP, isolating White's QRP and creating a new semi–hole, at White's QB5. White's queenside play is dead.

12. P–Q5 and 13. N–K1: After 11. . . . Q–K2 White had to protect his KP from the threat of 12. . . . PxP 13. NxP (13. QxP N–N5) NxP. With 12. P–Q5, however, White created another hole at his QB5, which Black might have been able to exploit later with . . . N–B4. White also gave up all chance of opening the Q–file with QPxKP after he advanced his QP. True, he could have continued

13. QPxBP, but that would have granted Black excellent queenside play against White's backward QNP along the QN-file. Note that after 13. QPxBP White would have gotten a good positional game with P–QN4–5 (securing Q5 as an outpost square) if the moves P–QR4/ . . . P–QR4 had not been played earlier. Thus, small positional errors add up to big concessions.

14. P–KN4?: After Black closed the queenside permanently, the only sector of the board to be opened was near the kings. Black had a natural advantage there because . . . P–KB4 was good for him, whereas P–KB4 would have been double-edged for White (since after . . . KPxBP Black could have set up an excellent outpost on his vacant K4 square). For this reason White played 14. P–KN4 with a view to establishing a solid bridge of pawns on K4, KB3, KN4, and KR3. But since Black could play . . . P–KR4 as well as . . . P–KB4, White's natural inferiority on the kingside had to be exposed. Again, had it not been for his earlier queenside errors, White might have been able to ignore the kingside and seize the initiative on the other side of the board.

17. KPxP? and *18. PxRP:* This was positional surrender since afterwards Black dominated the center and built up at will on the kingside. After this White had little counterplay in the center or on the queenside and could only await disaster on the KN- and KR-files. Black's positional edge made the final tactics possible.

Positional errors, as demonstrated above, are crimes against the pawn structure, the only static aspect of chess. Since pawns cannot move backwards, their advances have a great bearing on the performance of the other pieces—a bearing that is difficult to alter at a later stage. Pawn moves turn bishops from good pieces into spectators, weaken king positions, open dangerous lines for enemy pieces, create permanent weaknesses, and establish endgame advantages.

It can't be denied that sometimes a move is tactically good but positionally bad. Whether it is ultimately a good move or a bad one depends on the size and immediacy of the tactical advantages it confers. If it creates insurmountable threats, the move is good. But the attack may fail and the positional defects prove costly in the long run.

Position after 11. . . . NxB

Albin–Schiffers, Nuremberg 1896—*1. N–KB3 P–Q4 2. P–QN3 P–K3 3. B–N2 N–KB3 4. P–K3 P–B4 5. P–Q4 N–B3 6. QN–Q2 PxP 7. PxP B–Q3 8. N–K5 0–0 9. B–Q3 Q–B2! 10. P–KB4 N–QN5! 11. 0–0 NxB*

Accurate play has permitted Black to exchange a knight for White's better bishop. After 12. NxN P–QN3 or 12. . . . P–QN4 Black has excellent middlegame prospects because his two bishops have a much brighter future than White's knights.

12. PxN??

In the *short run*, there is a lot to be said for this move. White will gain control of the board's only open file with R–QB1. He will also be able to drive Black's knight away from kingside defense with P–KN4–5, now that . . . N–K5 is prohibited.

But the QB-file cannot be a permanent possession of White's. Nor should his kingside attack succeed against even a second-best defense. Once the short-run advantages are neutralized, Black should make the weak White pawns a decisive factor.

12. . . .	B–Q2
13. P–KN4	B–N4!
14. P–N5	N–Q2
15. R–B1	Q–Q1
16. QN–B3	P–B3!

This breaks the back of the attack and thus focuses attention on the weak pawns. The game ended relatively quickly.

17. PxP PxP 18. NxN QxN 19. P–QR4 B–R3 20. Q–Q2 Q–N2ch 21. K–R1 Q–R3 22. R–N1ch K–R1 23. R–N4 Q–R6! 24. R–N3 Q–B4! 25. R–Q1 BxBP 26. N–R4 Q–R4 27. QxB (desperation) QxRch 28. R–N1 Q–R4 29. R–N4 BxP 30. B–R3 B–K5ch 31. K–N1 QxRch White resigns (32. QxQ R–KN1).

Bad Bishops

Since the two players begin with two bishops each, any pawn move will affect one pair of bishops. But if bishops are traded off, for each other or for knights, the advance of pawns to squares controlled by the remaining bishops can be of major significance. If both sides have white-square bishops, for example, you should consider very carefully any advance that puts a pawn on a white square. Such an advance is doubly disadvantageous since it limits the scope of your bishop and creates a target for the enemy bishop.

Here is stark example of this common clerical crime.

Cohn–Spielmann, Karlsbad 1911—*1. P–K4 P–K3 2. P–Q4 P–Q4 3. N–QB3 N–KB3 4. PxP PxP 5. B–KN5 B–K2 6. B–Q3 N–QB3 7. KN–K2? N–QN5! 8. 0–0 0–0 9. N–N3 NxB 10. QxN P–B3 11. QR–K1 P–KR3 12. B–Q2 B–Q3 13. N–Q1 Q–B2*

Position after 13. . . . Q–B2

White's slight error at move 7 permitted Black to exchange off White's "good" bishop. It is good—while White's QB is "bad"—because there is a fixed White pawn on Q4, a black square.

White's remaining bishop, to be sure, is only slightly "bad" because only one White pawn, the QP, is stuck on a black square for the foreseeable future. But this changes with White's next move.

14. P–KB4?	B–Q2
15. Q–KB3	QR–K1
16. P–B3	B–KN5!

Black clearly understands the difference between good and bad bishops. He gets rid of his own bad bishop—bad because Black's fixed pawn is on a white square, Q4. He knows that in the later stages of the game White will be weak on the white squares and jumbled on the black ones. To ease the pressure White sought exchanges, but the trades only made the disadvantage of his bishop more evident.

17. Q–B2 BxN! 18. RxB N–K5 19. NxN RxN 20. QR–K1 KR–K1 21. P–KN3 (another black-square pawn, but White needed to support his KNP) *Q–R4 22. RxR RxR 23. P–QR3 Q–N4! 24. B–K3 Q–Q6 25. R–K1 P–KB4 26. Q–Q2 QxQ 27. BxQ K–B2 28. K–B2 K–B3 29. K–B3 P–KN4! 30. R–K2 K–N3*

White can't do much but sit and defend since RxR would give Black a powerful passed pawn. Meanwhile, Black is preparing 31. . . . K–R4 followed by 32. . . . RxR 33. KxR PxP and 34. . . . K–N5, winning a pawn and the game.

31. P–R3 P–N5ch! 32. PxP PxPch 33. K–B2 K–B4 34. B–K3 P–KR4 35. B–Q2 P–R5 36. RxR PxR 37. B–K3 P–QN4 (Now Black threatens to play . . . P–R6 and . . . K–K3–Q4–B5–N6 raiding the queenside against a hopeless bishop. On 38. PxP BxP 39. BxB KxB the king-and-pawn ending is easily won; e.g., 40. P–R5 K–N4 or 40. P–N3 P–N6ch 41. K–N2 P–K6.) *38. P–Q5 PxPch 39. KxP PxP 40. B–Q2 P–R4 41. P–QN4 P–R5 White resigns.*

Creating Holes

Another reason that 14. P–KB4 is bad in the game above is that it abandons pawn control of White's K4. After that pawn move Black could occupy the K5 square with a rook and pressure White into more weaknesses. He had a valuable hole for his pieces.

There are any number of excuses for creating pawn holes. "It was the only way to make my pieces active," or "I couldn't permit him to occupy the other square so I gave him this one," and so on. Sometimes you get drawn into a very bad, hole-ruined position by making natural-looking moves. This is what happened to Black below:

Petrosian–Larsen, Beverwijk 1960—*1. P–QB4 P–Q3 2. P–Q4 P–K4 3. N–KB3 N–Q2 4. N–B3 KN–B3 5. P–K4 B–K2 6. B–K2 0–0 7. 0–0 P–B3 8. P–Q5*

Position after 8. P–Q5

Compare this position with the opening of Stoyko–Soltis at the start of this chapter. Here it is Black who must begin making difficult choices. White's P–Q5 is quite good here since he can continue with P–QN4 followed by QPxP and P–N5. That would eliminate Black's pawn control of his Q4 square and create a beautiful hole for White's pieces. It would also make Black's QP a permanent target along the Q-file.

Black may stop this plan with 8. . . . P–B4, but that has the drawback of encouraging P–QR3 and P–QN4 and the opening of a queenside file before Black is ready to contest it.

8. . . .   **N–B4?!**

This is double-edged since Black will be able to preserve his knight on QB4 only until it is driven out by P–QN4. Worse, Black's move encourages P–QN4 and makes . . . P–QB4 impossible.

9. N–Q2		**P–QR4**
10. P–QN3		**PxP?**

"From such a strong grandmaster it is impossible to expect such an antipositional move," annotator Salo Flohr said. Why antipositional? Because it completes the surrender of the queenside. To stop 10. P–QN4, Black played 9. . . . P–QR4. The only pawn left to protect Black's QN4 after . . . P–QR4 is the BP. But now after 10. . . . PxP that pawn is gone.

From Black's point of view it wasn't that simple. He didn't have an easy way of meeting 11. P–QR3 12. R–N1 and 13. P–QN4, so he played 10. . . . PxP in the hope of using the QB-file for counterplay. But watch what happens.

11. BPxP		**B–Q2**
12. P–QR4!		

This stops 12. . . . P–QN4 and thereby ensures that both QN5 *and* QB4 will be outpost holes for White. If White puts a knight on QB4 he will threaten both the Black QP and QRP. And if Black protects the RP with . . . P–QN3, he creates a new hole at his QB3. Holes beget holes.

The White superiority is disguised here, but it becomes evident after *12. . . . Q–N3 13. B–R3 KR–B1 14. R–N1 Q–R2 15. R–B1 R–B2 16. B–N5! B–N5* (Black knows about good and bad bishops) *17. Q–K1! N–R3 18. P–R3 B–R4 19. BxN! QxB 20. N–B4.*

Here White's strategy has succeeded completely: Black's pieces are out of play and his QB-file is neatly plugged up. If he sits and waits, White wins; e.g., 20. . . . N–K1 21. N–N5 R(2)–B1 22. NxKP! or 20. . . . R–Q2 21. N–N5 B–B1 22. Q–K3 followed by N–N6 or just the doubling of rooks on the QB-file. This pessimistic future explains *20. . . . RxN,* but Black never has enough compensation and loses eventually after *21. PxR QxP 22. P–B3 N–K1 23. Q–K2 Q–Q5ch 24. K–R1 B–N4 25. KR–Q1 Q–N3 26. R–QN1 Q–B2 27. N–N5.*

Holes need not be unoccupied squares such as Black's QN4 and QB5 in the last game. Sometimes you discover that a square which seems to be strong because you have a pawn on it is really vulnerable because it can't be controlled permanently by other pawns and pieces. In the following game it turns out that White's QB4 is a hole in disguise. White's biggest error is the failure to protect the masked hole with pieces.

Landau–Alekhine, Kemeri 1937—*1. P–Q4 P–K3 2. P–QB4 B–N5ch 3. N–B3 P–KB4 4. Q–N3 Q–K2 5. P–QR3 BxNch 6. QxB N–KB3 7. N–B3 N–B3 8. P–QN4?! P–Q3 9. B–N2 B–N2 10. P–N3? N–K5 11. Q–N3 P–QR4! 12. P–N5 P–R5! 13. Q–B2 N–R4!*

Position after 13. . . . N–R4

White may not appreciate it yet but he has a big problem brewing on his QB4. Sometimes you will read the comment "It's not only the pawn that is weak but the square." That sounds mysterious, since squares alone don't win chess games. But here we see White being punished for the surrender of pawn control of QB4 (8. P–QN4 gave up the chance of a subsequent P–QN3) and the development of his KB on a diagonal that fails to meet the problem of QB4. White may not lose the QBP since he can advance it. But he will certainly lose the QB4 square.

Now he can't play 14. P–K3 because of 14. . . . N–N4. Probably best is 14. QxP N–Q3! 15. P–B5, although Black wins back his pawn at will (plus a continuing positional advantage) after 15. . . . N(3)–B5.

| **14. B–N2?** | **N–Q3** |
| **15. P–B5** | **N(3)–B5!** |

This is better than 15. . . . NxP since Black can grab a pawn at a later point while maintaining an iron grip on B5. Black's pieces would become a little uncoordinated after 15. . . . NxP. Now they cripple the queenside.

16. PxP PxP 17. 0–0 QR–B1! 18. B–B3 (the threat was 18. . . . N–K6) *N–N6 19. B–N4* (or 19. R–R2 NxRP) *P–Q3 20. QR–B1* (else 20. . . . N–K6) *0–0 21. Q–R2 NxR 22. RxN N–K4*, and Black simplified into a won endgame.

Accepting Backward Pawns

Backward pawns are pawns that cannot advance because of imminent capture by an enemy pawn and cannot be protected by friendly pawns. Technically we only consider a pawn to be backward when it can be attacked along the file in front of it. For example, if Black has pawns on Q3 and K4, facing pawns at White's K4 and QB4, the Black QP is backward. (If there were a White pawn at his Q5, the Black QP would not be subject to attack along the Q-file and wouldn't be "backward.")

Such a pawn subjects the defender to a burdensome task of protection and interferes with his piece coordination. Nobody likes that, but there are times when it is justified. The problem is to determine what constitutes sufficient justification.

Duras–Chajes, Karlsbad 1911—*1. P–Q4 P–Q4 2. N–KB3 P–K3 3. P–B4 N–KB3 4. P–K3 P–B3 5. B–Q3 QN–Q2 6. 0–0 B–Q3 7. N–B3 0–0 8. P–K4 PxKP 9. NxP NxN 10. BxN P–KB4?*

Position after 10. . . . P–KB4

Black's last move is extremely weakening because it concedes all pawn control of his K4 (a hole) and makes the KP a permanent backward target until he can play . . . P–K4. White has three middlegame themes to work with: *(a)* occupation of K5; *(b)* attack against the KP; and *(c)* preparation for P–Q5, which would open lines leading to the Black king now that . . . P–KB4 has loosened the king's pawn protection. All that Black gets out of 10. . . . P–B4 is a one-move retreat of White's bishop from K4.

11. B–B2	N–B3
12. Q–K2	P–QN3
13. P–QN3!	

White develops his bishop on a square that *(a)* restrains . . . P–K4, the move Black needs to "repair" his backward KP, and (b) aims at the kingside in case White's QP gets to advance.

13. . . .	P–QR4
14. B–N2	Q–B2
15. QR–Q1	R–K1
16. KR–K1	B–N2
17. P–B5!	

White might have prepared for a different attack, such as P–KR3 and N–N5. But 17. P–B5 breaks the game open; e.g., 17. . . . PxP 18. PxP BxP 19. Q–B4!, winning at least a pawn.

17. . . .	B–KB1
18. N–N5	B–B1
19. BxP!	

This bishop can't be taken because of 20. Q–B4ch K–R1 (20. . . . N–Q4 21. RxR) 21. N–B7ch K–N1 22. RxR NxR 23. N–R6ch with mate. It's fitting now that Black loses both his backward KP and the pawn that made its brother backward. The game went 42 moves, but Black was doomed after *19. . . . P–R3 20. BxPch BxB 21. NxB.*

There are times when it is necessary to create a backward pawn in order to obtain freedom for your pieces. But then you have to keep alert for the opportunity to liquidate the weak pawn. If you don't, your dearly purchased freedom may be short-lived, and you will spend the rest of the game protecting that weakling.

Averbakh–Petrosian, Leningrad 1960—*1. P–Q4 N–KB3 2. P–QB4 P–KN3 3. P–KN3 B–N2 4. B–N2 0–0 5. N–KB3 P–Q3 6. 0–0 P–QR3 7. N–B3 N–B3 8. P–Q5 N–QR4 9. N–Q2 P–B4 10. Q–B2 P–K4!? 11. PxP e.p. BxP 12. P–N3*

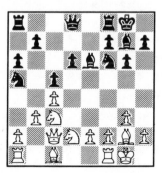

Position after 12. P–N3

You can't blame Black's subsequent loss on 10. . . . P–K4. His bid for activity in the center was justified by White's slow maneuvering (Q–B2 and N–Q2). That maneuvering would be appropriate with a closed center, but with a slightly opened center Black should at least be able to equalize.

Note that 11. . . . BxP is better than 11. . . . PxP since Black activates his pieces much faster with the bishop capture and is able to dissolve his pawn weakness. (But after 11. . . . PxP and a subsequent . . . P–Q4 Black would still have a weak KP to worry about.)

12. . . .   **N–B3?!**

This is a reasonable move, but Black's temporary initiative should have been used to repair his weakness with 12. . . . P–Q4!. Black's lead in development enables him to trade off his weak QP; e.g., 13. PxP NxQP 14. NxN BxN 15. BxB? BxR or 14. B–N2 N(R)–B3.

13. B–N2   **N–QN5?**

Again Black misses his chance for 13. . . . P–Q4! (e.g., 14. PxP NxP 15. NxN BxB 16. QxB BxN or 15. QN–K4 N–Q5).

14. Q–B1   **Q–K2?!**

This was the last moment for . . . P–Q4. On 14. . . . P–Q4 15. P–QR3 N–B3 16. PxP NxP 17. QN–K4! N–Q5 18. R–K1 White retains a slight edge but it is nothing to write home about.

15. QN–K4!

With this White puts an end to . . . P–Q4 because Black's QBP would become too weak after QPxP. This is how one bad pawn spreads gloom over the rest of the board.

There is a great deal of play left in the game, but its basic tenor is already set by the 15th move. White will be able to occupy the Q5 hole and attack the backward QP now that he has equalized development. By piling up against the QP, White distracts Black from other potential targets and eventually breaks through on the kingside.

15 . . . NxN 16. NxN KR–Q1 17. R–Q1 QR–N1 18. R–Q2 R–Q2 19. BxB KxB 20. Q–N2ch P–B3 21. QR–Q1 QR–Q1 21. N–B3! N–B3 23. N–Q5 BxN (the bad pawn forces Black to concede White a better minor piece since he couldn't meet 23. . . . Q–B2 24. N–N6) *24. RxB Q–K3 25. P–K3 P–QN4 26. Q–K2 N–K2 27. R(5)–Q2 R–QN1 28. B–Q5 Q–R6 29. Q–B3! PxP 30. BxP R–N3 31. Q–R8!* (threatening Q–K8) *Q–B4 32. P–K4 Q–N5 33. Q–K8 P–Q4* (twenty moves too late) *34. BxP NxB 35. PxN QR–Q3 36. R–K1 K–R3 37. R–K4 Q–B6 38. R–R4ch K–N4* (38. . . . K–N2 39.

R–K2 R–KB2 40. RxPch!) *39. Q–KB8 P–B4 40. R–KB4 Q–B6 41.
P–R4ch K–R4 42. RxPch K–N5 43. P–B3ch and Black resigned*
in view of 43. . . . KxP 44. R–N5ch.

Opening Lines for Enemy Pieces

Even when pawns move without compromising your pieces or
weakening themselves or other pawns, these advances can help
the enemy. They may give him a vital open line for pieces that
previously had little future.

Schlechter–Tchigorin, Ostende 1907—*1. P–K4 P–K4 2. N–KB3
N–QB3 3. B–N5 P–QR3 4. B–R4 N–B3 5. 0–0 B–K2 6. R–K1
P–QN4 7. B–N3 P–Q3 8. P–B3 0–0 9. P–KR3 N–QR4 10. B–B2
P–B4 11. P–Q4 Q–B2 12. QN–Q2 BPxP 13. PxP B–Q2 14. N–B1
N–B3 15. B–K3 N–QN5 16. B–N1 KR–B1 17. Q–Q2!*

Position after 17. Q–Q2

This is typical of the kind of position that arises from the popular
Ruy Lopez opening. Whether you play this opening or not, you
can appreciate the nature of the middlegame battle. With a some-
what closed center Black's slight edge in development isn't significant. White parries Black's threats (17. . . . . N–B7? 18. R–B1)
and is ready to take over the initiative after N–N3, P–QR3, B–Q3,
and QR–B1.

All of this suggests that Black should open some lines for his
pieces. But this would be bad thinking. His pieces are not par-
ticularly well centralized and would not profit from an opening

of the center. White's pieces, especially his knights and white-square bishop, would. This explains Black's rapid downfall.

17. . . .	**P–Q4?**
18. **N–N3**	**KPxP?**
19. **BxP**	**PxP**
20. **BxN!**	**BxB**
21. **NxP**	

With the liquidation of the center Black's game falls apart. He might have been able to compete if he had placed his rooks at Q1 and K1 and posted his QB at QN2. But here Black has little strength mustered in the center and nothing with which to defend his kingside.

21. . . .	**B–K2**
22. **N(4)–N5**	

Now Black might try 22. . . . BxN 23. NxB P–KR3 but then 24. NxP KxN 25. QxN would leave him helpless and a pawn down to boot. Black's collapse was swift now since both K2 and KR2 were vulnerable to White's suddenly active pieces.

22. . . . N–B3 23. BxPch K–B1 24. QR–Q1 R–Q1 25. NxP! B–KB4 (25. . . . KxN 26. Q–Q5ch and 26. . . . K–B1 27. Q–N8 mate or 26. . . . K–B3 27. N–N5) 26. NxR RxN 27. QxRch! NxQ 28. BxB Q–N3 29. N–K5 K–N1 30. N–Q7 Q–R3 31. RxB Q–N4 32. N–B6ch Black resigns.

You can open lines for the enemy without offering exchanges of pawns. The advance of a pawn will in itself close certain lines and open others. In the following example we see Black with a substantial positional advantage because of his superior minor pieces, his control of the open QR-file, and the possible weakness of White's QP. But there is no clear way for Black to enlarge his edge.

Averbakh–Petrosian, Tiflis 1959
White to move

Just as one pawn weaknesss often leads to others, one open line can generate control of another. Here Black is ready to take control of the eighth rank with 1. . . . R–R8, but that alone won't win the game for him. With 1. P–KN3 and a subsequent K–N2 White can take the sting out of his concession of his first rank.

1. P–QN3??

The tactical point of this grave concession is to play R–QR4 at some point, exchanging off rooks and neutralizing most of Black's advantage. But White fails to see . . .

    1. . . .   **R–R7!**

Now White's position is ruined because he must go into contortions to protect his newly opened second rank. On 2. B–K2 Black starts off with 2. . . . NxP 3. QxN RxB.

    2. Q–K1   **Q–R4!**

This establishes a murderous pin and prepares to exploit it with 3. . . . B–Q7!. White must try to escape by means of tactics.

    3. Q–N1   **R–R8**
    4. R–N5

A queen move would permit 4. . . . QxR, and the attractive 4. R–R4 walks into the 4. . . . QxR desperado.

    4. . . .   **Q–B6!**

White's queen is mated, a direct result of his concession of the vital second rank.

Failure to Blockade or Restrain

Suppose you refuse to open any good lines for the enemy's pieces. That doesn't ensure against your opponent's making a pawn break that will open lines. It is a rare game in which a player, especially with White, is prevented from making any pawn break. But if you play accurately you can usually restrain the ones that will enable your opponent to dominate the key avenues of the board.

A typical method of restraint is the use of a blockader. By posting a piece, ideally a knight or bishop, in front of an enemy pawn you can mechanically stop the pawn from advancing. This is a typical situation.

Langeweb–Sosonko, Wijk aan Zee 1975
Black to move

White's piece placement is fairly unambitious. His QB is doing sentry duty on K3 rather than sitting on an aggressive square such as KN5. But his position is solid, and no attack on White's isolated pawn is likely to succeed. Black should not ignore that pawn, however. Even if it can't be captured it deserves attention because it can advance. At some later point P–Q5 would open up several central lines for White's pieces.

Therefore something like 1. . . . KR–Q1 is called for, followed by . . . B–KB1 and perhaps . . . N–K2–Q4. The last maneuver mentioned would bring Black's QN to an excellent post from which it stops P–Q5 and surveys such important squares as K6, QB6, and KB5.

1. . . .	QR–B1?!
2. Q–K2	N–KN5?
3. QR–Q1	NxB
4. QxN	

Black might be content here since he has no apparent weaknesses and has gained the advantage of a bishop over a knight. But he has given White time to centralize his heavy pieces and prepare for the break that can't be stopped. Since P–Q5 is coming, Black hastens to get out of the way. Too late.

4. . . .	Q–N1
5. P–Q5!	B–B4

After 5. . . . PxP 6. NxP KR–K1 7. N–N5! Black has too many problems on the kingside because of White's open lines; e.g., 7. . . . B–B1 8. Q–Q3 P–N3 9. N–B6ch or 7. . . . P–KR3 8. NxBP KxN 9. discovered check.

6. Q–Q3	PxP
7. NxP	KR–K1

On 7. . . . P–KR3 White would win with 8. N–B6ch PxN 9. Q–N6ch using the diagonal pin. After 7. . . . KR–K1 White could win with 8. N–N5 but he took a little longer: *8. RxRch RxR 9. B–N1 P–B4 10. QxP P–N3 11. Q–B6! R–KB1 12. Q–B3 N–K4 13. B–R2,* and Black gave up in short order.

Advancing Kingside Pawns

A special case of pawn errors that don't (*a*) create pawn targets or (*b*) compromise your pieces and yet are among the most damaging of positional mistakes is the careless advance of your kingside pawns. A slight weakness on a queenside square may not be worth worrying about. But a thoughtless P–KN4 or P–KB3 can quickly bring down your whole position. The reason should be obvious: the kings are usually found on the kingside.

Yet such moves as P–KN4, what Siegbert Tarrasch called "the hari-kari move," are played all the time, even by the best of players. Sometimes we hope to open up the enemy pawn structure with exchanges and checkmate before our own king weakness becomes apparent. Or we play such a move to restrict enemy pieces or to obtain some other positional advantage. There are many reasons.

Ragozin–Botvinnik, Match 1941—*1. P–K4 P–K3 2. P–Q4 P–Q4 3. N–Q2 P–QB4 4. KN–B3 N–QB3 5. KPxP KPxP 6. B–N5 PxP 7. 0–0 B–Q3 8. N–N3 KN–K2 9. QNxP P–KR3 10. B–K3 0–0 11. Q–Q2 B–KN5 12. B–K2 R–B1 13. QR–Q1 B–N1 14. P–KR3 B–R4*

Position after 14. . . . B–R4

White's downfall in this game comes from a purely voluntary weakening of his kingside. He has completed his development and looks for a plan. Suppose I play 15. NxN, he asks himself. Then if he recaptures with a knight he loses his QP, and if he takes with his rook I can play N–Q4 with good pressure against the enemy QP. On the third possibility, 15. NxN PxN, I can harass his queenside with B–QR6 and batter his center with P–QB4.

15. NxN   **PxN**
16. P–KN4?

White thinks he needs this because on 16. B–QR6 Black can ruin the kingside with 16. . . . BxN. But White's kingside is also weakened by the text move since the QN8–KR2 diagonal can never be blocked by P–KN3. The more modest 16. B–B5 and P–QB4 was called for.

| 16. . . . | B–N3 |
| 17. B–R6 | Q–Q3! |

Exactly. White cannot get away with such a cavalier attitude toward his kingside. On 18. BxR B–K5 White is helpless against 19. . . . BxN and 20. . . . Q–R7ch.

| 18. KR–K1 | B–K5! |
| 19. Q–K2 | N–N3 |

There was no immediate win with 19. . . . BxN 20. QxB Q–R7ch 21. K–B1, but now 20. . . . N–R5 is threatened and . . . P–KB4 is always available. White collapsed with:

20. K–B1 QR–K1 21. N–N1 P–KB4! 22. PxP N–R5! 23. Q–N4 NxP 24. P–KB3, and he resigned before Black could play 24. . . . BxKBP 25. NxB NxBch.

A frequent delusion that lures players into weakening their kingside is the belief that they have a monopoly on the attack. Everyone is brave when he holds the initiative.

Golombek–Kottnauer, Prague 1946
Black to move

Although a pawn behind Black had missed the coup de grâce earlier. Now he wants to finish the game off quickly. The correct way is 1. . . . Q–KN8 followed by capturing the KRP and promoting Black's advanced pawn. On 1. . . . Q–KN8 2. K–B3 Black can play the aggressive 2. . . . P–N4, not just to open lines but to play 3. . . . P–N5ch.

1. . . .   P–N4??

This seems just as good as 1. . . . Q–KN8 since White dare not take this pawn (2. PxP Q–KN8!).

2. P–Q4!

But now White's king can escape, and it turns out that . . . P–KN4 has made the Black king a more vulnerable target.

2. . . . Q–R8 3. K–Q3 Q–B6ch 4. R–K3 QxP 5. Q–K2 R–Q1 (here 5. . . . Q–B7 6. QxQ! RxQ 7. KxP P–N5 8. P–Q5 would prove White's pawn was faster) 6. R–K4 Q–B8 7. Q–N4! Q–Q7ch 8. K–B4 (and now 8. . . . P–B7 would lose to 9. Q–K6ch K–N2 10. Q–K7ch and 11. R–K6ch, another illustration of the evil of 1. . . . P–N4??) 8. . . . R–KB1 9. R–K5 P–B7 10. RxPch Black resigns.

Another form of this error arises when a defender believes it necessary to advance a kingside pawn to strengthen his fortress. But each advance creates the opportunity for a new pawn break.

In the following case Black sees the threat to his KN2 after 13. R–N3. But with 13. . . . KR–Q1 and 14. . . . B–B1! Black would establish a rock-solid kingside without compromising his pawns. Instead, 13. . . . P–KN3 makes the P–KR5 break possible.

Schlechter–Teichmann, Nuremberg 1896—*1. P–K4 P–Q4 2. PxP QxP 3. N–QB3 Q–QR4 4. P–Q4 P–QB3 5. N–B3 B–N5 6. B–K2 N–B3 7. 0–0 P–K3 8. N–K5 BxB 9. QxB B–K2 10. B–N5 0–0 11. QR–Q1 Q–B2 12. R–Q3 QN–Q2 13. R–N3 P–KN3? 14. P–KR4! K–N2 15. P–R5 NxN* (15. . . . NxN 16. QxN! PxQ 17. BxBch K–R1 18. NxN or 17. . . . K–R3 18. B–N5ch) *16. PxN N–N1 17. B–K3! QR–Q1 18. P–B4! N–R3 19. R–R3 N–B4 20. B–B2 Q–R4 21. P–KN4! N–R3 22. K–R1 R–Q2 23. B–K3 B–B4 24. B–B1 N–N1 25. Q–R2! KR–Q1 26. PxP BPxP* (26. . . . RPxP 27. R–R8!) *27. RxPch K–B1 28. P–B5 Q–R3 29. R–K1 Black resigns.*

Permitting Pawn Majorities and Passed Pawns

About once a game the choice between two pawn recaptures occurs. Most of the time there is one clearly superior method. If, for example, you can capture material on your KN3 with either your pawn at KR2 or your pawn at KB2, it is usually best to choose the RP. In this way you move your pawn mass toward the center where it will count more heavily.

But there are many exceptions to the capture-toward-the-center rule. The two most important exceptions arise when you are helping the enemy establish a passed pawn or creating a pawn majority for him.

Tarrasch–Michel, Semmering 1926
Black to move

White has just played 1. BxN(Q5) in order to reduce the position to good knight vs. bad bishop. Black may not be happy about 1. . . . KPxB 2. N–B5 which gives White control over the K-file. But *1. . . . BPxB??* is much worse. White would have no clear method of winning after 1. . . . KPxB. But the other capture, although "toward the center," creates a majority of White pawns on the queenside. White then wins by using his passed pawn as a threat:

2. P–QN4 R–Q1 3. R–QB1 PxP 4. NPxP Q–R4 5. Q–B3! QxQ 6. RxQ R–B2 7. R–N3 B–B3 8. P–B4 (to stop . . . P–K4) *K–B1 9. KR–N1 K–K2 10. K–B2 P–KR4 11. R–N8! R(2)–Q2 12. K–N3*

P–B3 13. R–B8! RxR 14. NxRch K–B2 15. R–N3 R–B2 16. N–Q6ch
K–N3 17. R–K3 B–Q2 18. P–B5ch! PxP 19. R–K7! P–B5ch 20.
KxP, and Black resigned because the passed pawn (21. P–B6!)
will win a piece.

Strategic Errors

Someone once defined tactics as "what to do when there's something to do." Strategy, on the other hand, is "what to do when there's nothing to do." For a good part of an average chess game there is very little to do, at least tactically. Strategic play may seem to be even rarer, but it forms the spine for the body of middlegame play.

Choosing the right strategic plan is a vital chore. Too often we take planning for granted, choosing a particular policy—attack on the kingside, thrust in the center, etc.—because we've played that way in this kind of position before. It's when we choose a bad plan that we take notice.

And we must choose a plan. Waiting tactics are generally to be avoided. Few opening systems permit you to survive just by exchanging material or "passing."

Chukaev–Averbakh, U.S.S.R. 1959—1. P–Q4 N–KB3 2. P–QB4 P–K3 3. N–KB3 P–Q4 4. PxP PxP 5. B–N5 P–B3 6. Q–B2 B–K2 7. P–K3 N–K5 8. BxB QxB 9. N–B3 B–B4 10. B–Q3 N–Q2 11. 0–0 0–0 12. N–Q2? NxN(7) 13. QxN BxB 14. QxB P–KB4! 15. N–K2 N–N3 16. Q–B3 P–N4! 17. KR–K1 QR–K1 18. N–N3 N–B5 19. N–B1 Q–B3 20. P–QN3 N–Q3 21. QR–Q1 R–K3 22. N–Q2 R(1)–K1 23. N–B3 N–B2 24. Q–Q3 P–N5! 25. N–Q2 P–B5! 26. N–B1 N–N4 27. N–Q2 P–B6 28. Q–B1 Q–B4 29. R–B1 PxP 30. QxP N–R6ch 31. K–B1 RxP! and White resigned.

White didn't seem to do anything wrong but he lost. Actually he lost because he didn't seem to do anything period. At move 12 he could have chosen a queenside attack with QR–N1 and P–QN4–5, central play in preparation for P–K4, or something else. He might have tried the queenside idea a few moves later despite the loss of time. But by move 21 Black was winning, slowly but surely. Black had a good plan—kingside attack—whereas White had none.

Neglect of Center

Before you begin planning you must be secure in the center. This is the bare minimum of strategic decision-making.

You don't need a model center, with two or three healthy pawns on center squares. You may not need any pawns at all in the middle of the board. What you need is assurance that your opponent won't be able to dominate the center. If the center is closed by a mass of immobile pawns you are free to indulge in the lengthiest of maneuvers on the wings (such as on p. 178). But if the center is partially open and you have little control over its squares, there is no time for wing strategies.

After the opening moves *1. P–Q4 N–KB3 2. P–QB4 P–KN3 3. N–QB3 B–N2 4. P–K4 P–Q3 5. N–B3 0–0 6. B–B4,* White has an ostensible superiority in the center because he has three pawns there whereas Black has none. But Black has the potential to fight back in the center. For example, with 6. . . . B–N5 7. B–K2 N–B3 he is ready to neutralize the center with 8. . . . BxN 9. BxB P–K4!.

If Black neglects the center, however, he turns the most valuable real estate on the board over to White; e.g., *6. . . . P–KR3? 7. Q–Q2 K–R2 8. P–KR3 QN–Q2 9. 0–0–0 P–N3? 10. P–K5!*

Position after 10. P–K5

White is not ready to break through in the center decisively since a general exchange of pawns there would give Black's pieces back their scope. But with the assurance that he faces no counterplay in the center, White can prepare for attack, say on the kingside, with complete confidence.

Siegbert Tarrasch was a turn-of-the-century German master whose teachings revolutionized chess strategy. Yet Tarrasch once held this position as Black (vs. Bogolyubov, Karlsbad 1923) and lost miserably after *10. . . . N–KN1 11. B–Q3 B–N2 12. B–K4! BxB 13. NxB Q–B1 14. Q–B2 Q–R3 15. K–N1 K–R1 16. P–KR4 QR–Q1 17. P–R5 QPxP 18. QPxP P–QN4 19. BPxP QxP 20. PxP PxP 21. N–R4! NxP (21. . . . RxB 22. NxPch K–R2 23. N–N5 mate) 22. BxN BxB 23. NxPch K–N2 24. NxR RxN 25. R–R3 N–B3 26. R–QN3 Q–R3 27. N–B5 Q–B3 28. R–K1 Black resigns.*

Tarrasch, more than anyone of his generation, knew that a wing attack (*14. . . . Q–R3, 18. . . . P–QN4*) could not succeed with an inferior center. But, having lost the battle of the center by the 10th move, there were no good plans for him.

That game was played at a time of great controversy over the value of pawn centers. One school of thought, the Hypermoderns, held that advanced pawns, even in the center, only provided the enemy with targets. The Classicists argued that a secure center was a source of strength, not weakness. (Tarrasch, ironically, was the foremost Classicist.)

Today we know that the vital element in the center controversy is the scope of pieces. If your pawn center gives you plenty of piece play, it is an advantage. If there is no pawn center to speak of, your highest priority is controlling the pawnless squares.

For example, after *1. P–Q4 N–KB3 2. P–QB4 P–KN3 3. N–QB3 B–N2 4. P–K4 P–Q3 5. N–B3 0–0 6. B–K2 P–K4 7. 0–0 N–B3 8. B–K3 R–K1! 9. P–Q5 N–Q5! 10. NxN PxN 11. BxP NxKP 12. BxB KxB 13. NxN RxN*, a superficial look may lead to the conclusion that White is better.

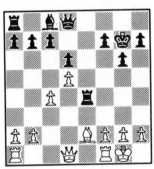

Position after 13. . . . RxN

"After all," White might say, "I can kick the Black rook backwards and then choose between attack on the weakened kingside and advance on the queenside with P–B5."

"Not at all," Black would reply. "Your pieces are inferior to mine in terms of center control, and your wing attacks therefore won't work. I can put my bishop on B4 and queen on B3. What can your pieces do?"

Black is right. The position favors him slightly, whether in the middlegame or ending (e.g., *14. B–Q3 R–K1 15. Q–B3 Q–B3 16. QxQch KxQ 17. KR–K1 B–Q2 18. P–QN3? RxRch 19. RxR R–K1 20. RxR BxR 21. K–B1 K–K4 22. K–K2 K–Q5* with a graphic example of central domination extending into the endgame).

A good example of what may happen in the middlegame if White neglects the center is Ilivitsky-Suetin, Kiev 1954, which went *14. R–B1? Q–B3 15. B–B3 R–Q5! 16. Q–N3 P–N3 17. Q–R4?* (17. KR–Q1 is best to neutralize the center) *B–B4 18. P–QN4 P–QR4 19. P–QR3 R–Q6.*

Black already has a winning threat of *20. . . . RxB 21. PxR*

B–R6. The finish was remarkably quick—though not that remarkable considering Black's tremendous centralized power.

20. *B–K2 R–Q7 21. B–B3* (21. Q–B6 RxB! 22. QxR B–K5 and . . . Q–N4) *21. . . . Q–N7 22. P–B5 RxBP! 23. Q–B6 RxB! 24. QxR R–K6* (threatens 25 . . . R–K7 and . . . B–K5) *25. Q–Q8 R–K7 26. Q–N5 P–R3 27. Q–N3 B–K5 White resigns.*

Playing on the Wrong Side

The first decision in planning is a choice of the area of the board on which to concentrate one's pieces and attention. Some rare positions offer good prospects whether you attack on the kingside, queenside, or in the center. But in most cases there is a good way and a bad way to play.

Taimanov–Averbakh, Moscow 1958—*1. P–Q4 N–KB3 2. P–QB4 P–K3 3. N–QB3 B–N5 4. P–B3 P–Q4 5. P–QR3 BxNch 6. PxB 0–0 7. PxP PxP 8. P–K3 N–R4 9. N–K2 P–KB4 10. P–QB4 P–B3 11. Q–N3 K–R1 12. K–B2 PxP 13. QxBP N–Q2 14. N–B3 N–N3 15. Q–B5 B–K3 16. R–QN1 N–B3 17. B–K2 KN–Q4 18. NxN BxN 19. R–Q1*

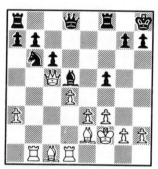

Position after 19. R–Q1

White's unusual method of bringing his king to safety has worked out fairly well, and both sides are about to complete their development. White will have a choice between two plans: playing on the queenside with P–QR4–5 and thrusting in the center with P–K4. But what about Black?

He has no effective pawn break since . . . P–KB5 will be met by P–K4 and . . . P–QB4 will require too much preparation. Therefore Black will have to work with his pieces against the pawn structure he faces right now. With that in mind it seems unlikely he will be able to achieve anything immediate in the center. But 19. . . . Q–Q2 followed by 20. . . . QR–K1 is still a reasonable method of continuing.

Another possible plan is 19. . . . Q–R5ch! 20. K–N1 QR–K1 followed by . . . R–B3–R3. Anytime you choose a kingside attack you must determine whether you can be upset by a central counterattack. But with a Black queen on KR5 and a rook on K1, White will not have enough power to make P–K4 effective.

The third plan, and the least effective, was:

19. . . .	N–R5?
20. Q–B2	P–QN4
21. K–N1	N–N3

Black has opted to restrain White from queenside play and to create his own pressure there with . . . N–B5, . . . Q–K2, and perhaps . . . P–QR4 and . . . P–N5.

22. P–K4!

But Black didn't take this counterstroke sufficiently into consideration. Black's choice of target areas—the queenside—leads to a massive White advance in the center.

22. . . . B–B5 23. P–Q5! BxB 24. QxB PxKP 25. BPxP N–B5 26. B–K3! Q–K2 (Black must lose material after 26. . . . NxB 27. QxN PxP 28. RxNP) *27. B–Q4! PxP 28. RxP KR–Q1* (or 28. . . . Q–KP 29. QxQ PxQ 30. R–N7 R–KN1 31. B–B3 and 32. R(1)–Q7) *29. R–K1 QxKP? 30. Q–KB2!*, and Black resigned because of White's impending doubling of rooks on the seventh rank.

Onesidedness

Having found a good plan on the right side you can still go wrong by concentrating entirely on it to the detriment of the other sectors of the board. There is a dangerous tendency to mentally divide the board into "my side" and "his side," ignoring developments on the opposite wing while you devote your energies to following through with the plan on "your" side.

Keene–Stein, Hastings 1967/68—*1. N–KB3 P–Q3. 2. P–B4 N–KB3 3. P–KN3 P–KN3 4. B–N2 B–N2 5. 0–0 0–0 6. N–B3 P–K4 7. P–Q3 N–B3 8. R–N1 P–KR3 9. P–QN4 B–K3 10. P–N5 N–K2 11. Q–B2?! Q–Q2*

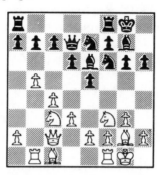

Position after 11. . . . Q–Q2

White follows a policy from here on of directing his attention to his left. He makes his first and last significant kingside step now with *12. R–K1?* preparing to meet *12. . . . B–R6* with *13. B–R1*. White wants to keep his white-square bishop because it is part of his antiqueenside artillery and because it protects so many key squares around his king. Had he given more consideration to Black's side of the board, the kingside, he would have accomplished the same goal of bishop preservation with *12. R–Q1!* and also retained the prospect of meeting a flank attack on the king wing with P–Q4!.

Yet White—"naively" as the loser put it—assumed that the outcome of the game depended on which attack created the greatest and quickest damage, White's on the queenside or Black's on the kingside. There followed *12. . . . B–R6 13. B–R1 N–N5 14. N–Q2 QR–N1 15. N–Q5 NxN 16. PxN.*

White could also recapture on the Q5 square with a bishop, but then Black could demonstrate that both players have a stake on the queenside by playing *16. BxN P–QB3 17. PxP PxP.* Instead,

White stops . . . P–QB3 and prepares to pound at QB7 along the QB-file.

After *16. . . . P–KB4*, however, Black can cover his QB2 target with a rook and then turn all his attention to the kingside. Once Black has established a secure queenside—taking the even-handed approach to the middlegame that White disdained—he can take his time on the kingside (such as with . . . P–KN4 and . . . Q–B2–R4) or in the center (. . . P–K5).

White, a bit discouraged at this point, made some belated efforts to watch both wings of the board *(17. R–N4 QR–K1 18. N–B3 N–B3 19. P–K4*—to stop 19. . . . P–K5) but ended up losing because of weaknesses throughout the position: *19. . . . P–B5 20. B–QN2 N–N5 21. R–B4 R–K2 22. P–R4 R(2)–B2 23. Q–K2 Q–Q1 24. R–B2 P–KR4 25. B–B1 B–R3 26. B–QN2 PxP 27. RPxP P–R5 28. B–B1 PxP 29. PxP BxB 30. R(1)xB P–R3! 31. N–R2—* the threat was . . . Q–R1–R2ch!—*NxN 32. KxN Q–N4! 33. KxB R–R2ch 34. K–N2 Q–R3 and White resigned.*

Another defect of the onesided approach to planning is that only a few pawn structures permit a player to assume proprietary control over a wing. In most middlegames both players have at least some chances on each side of the board and in the center. There is competition in all sectors.

Soltis–Anderson, Phoenix 1978—*1. P–K4 P–QB4 2. N–KB3 N–QB3 3. P–Q4 PxP 4. NxP N–B3 5. N–QB3 P–K4 6. KN–N5 P–Q3 7. N–Q5 NxN 8. PxN N–N1 9. P–QB4 P–QR3 10. N–B3 B–K2 11. B–Q3 0–0 12. 0–0 P–B4 13. P–B3 N–Q2 14. B–K3*

Position after 14. B–K3

This is the starting point for strategy since both players are nearly finished with their development. White prefers to play on the queenside, where he has a numerical majority of pawns and an effective pawn break with P–QB5. Black's choice is more difficult. If he continues routinely (14. . . . N–B3 15. P–QN4 B–Q2 16. Q–N3 K–R1 17. QR–B1 R–B1) White will accomplish his goal (P–B5) before Black can even hint at counterplay.

Just from hearing a description of White's strategy you should know that Black's interests are likely to lie in the center and on the kingside. He could generate some activity with 14. . . . B–N4!, for example. That would seek an exchange of Black's bad bishop —a positional idea—and also advance a strategic goal (by gaining space on the kingside, by weakening K6, and by permitting Black to seize the initiative on the queenside with . . . Q–N3 once the bishops are exchanged). Of course, White can—and should —retreat the bishop, 15. B–KB2, but Black would have gained space for himself with 14. . . . B–N4. He can seek kingside weaknesses for a later attack (15. . . . B–R5 16. P–KN3 B–N4) or prepare for play in the center with the pawn sacrifice of 15. . . . P–K5 16. PxP P–B5! followed by . . . N–K4 and . . . B–N5 or . . . P–B6.

14. . . .	Q–K1?!
15. P–QN4	P–B5?
16. B–KB2	Q–R4

Black has chosen a bad plan. He is right to look toward the kingside but wrong to compromise his center (giving away K5 to White's minor pieces) and pieces (making his KB worse) in order to threaten 17. . . . R–B3 and 18. . . . R–R3.

His decision was prompted by a simple practical concern: he didn't see how White could possibly defend his kingside now. White cannot cover his KR2 sufficiently (17. K–R1 R–B3 18. B–KN1 R–R3 19. N–K4 B–R5! and 20. . . . N–B3 followed by . . . B–N6) and cannot survive a bishop sacrifice on KR3 if he tries to shield his king by advancing his KRP. Also, on 17. N–K4 Black can play 17. . . . N–B3 18. P–B5 NxN 19. BxN R–B3 with 20. . . . R–R3 coming up.

17. P–B5	R–B3
18. P–N4!	

Black never considered such a defense, and yet it demolishes his attack in a few moves. Black ruled it out of consideration because he believed the kingside was his turf. Having determined that his attack would come before White's queenside push, Black blinded himself to possible competition on the kingside.

18. . . . **PxP e.p.**

On 18. . . . Q–R6 White can choose between solid defense (19. K–R1 R–R3 20. B–KN1 holds now that White can defend along his second rank) or throwing Black's pieces into confusion (19. P–N5 R–B2 20. N–K4).

19. BxNP

White has purchased some room on the kingside for defense at the cost of a slight weakening. Black's strategy of mate on KR7 cannot succeed now (19. . . . R–R3 20. PxP B–R5 21. Q–K1), and his weakness in the center plus the lack of developed queenside pieces costs him the game.

19. . . . PxP 20. N–K4 R–R3 21. P–Q6 B–R5 (21. . . . BxP 22. NxB RxN 23. B–B4ch) 22. B–B4ch K–R1 23. Q–Q5! (counterattack in the center) Q–K1 24. BxB RxB 25. PxP N–B3 26. NxN PxN 27. Q–B7 QxQ 28. BxQ B–Q2 29. B–Q5 B–B3 30. BxB PxB 31. QR–N1 R–QB5 32. KR–B1 RxRch 33. RxR K–N2 34. R–N1 K–N3 35. R–N6 R–QB1? 36. RxBP! Black resigns.

Unjustified Attack

Black went in for a poor attack in this last example knowing that it was suspicious but not being able to foresee how White could defend himself. Most decisions to attack are made with different attitudes. Players decide to attack—be it on the kingside or queenside or in the center—when they feel their position warrants it. An experienced player will go further: "I didn't even like the idea of attacking. I wanted to play a quiet game today. But the position *demanded* that I attack."

When an attack is unjustified it is usually because of *(a)* inadequate development, *(b)* the availability of enemy counterattack, and *(c)* the absence of vulnerable targets. We've touched on the first two before. The last item is tricky and goes to the heart of

aggressive play. You can't attack if there is nothing to serve as
a target.

Drimer–Bronstein, Budapest 1961
White to move

Black's king looks a trifle awkward but his pieces are otherwise
well posted. What should White do? He can complete his development with B–K3 and R–Q1 and await events. But Black would
then be able to call the tune with . . . P–QR4 and . . . P–N5.
White could organize his men for play in the center (Q–K2,
R–Q3, B–K3, and QR–Q1). This would be a better idea than
waiting but is still relatively passive. There simply isn't any
aggressive play in the center since all the possible targets (Q6,
K5, K6) are well protected.

So White must look for a target or begin to think about going
on the defensive. An ideal way of meeting Black's . . . P–QN5
plan is 1. P–QN4!. Although this concedes the fine QB4 square
to Black's pieces, it threatens a queenside attack of White's own
with P–QR4.

1. P–KR4?

But there wasn't enough reason for continuing a kingside
attack. You might blame what now happens on the absence of
White's QR and QB from the kingside. Or you could say White's
collapse is due to Black's rapid seizure of open lines for counterplay. But the main reason for the result of this game is White's
misjudgment of the Black king's status. The king is actually quite

safe on KB2 with or without a pawn on KN4. It is not a true target.

1. . . .	**PxP!**
2. R–R3	**QR–KN1**

Meanwhile the White king turns out to be a target on KN1. Black takes over the KN-file and quickly restricts White to his second rank.

3. RxP P–KR4 4. Q–K2 R–N3 5. P–B3 R(1)–KN1 6. R–KR2 P–Q4 7. B–Q2 P–R5 8. RxP? (8. PxP PxP 9. QxP B–Q3 loses but 9. R–K1 would have put up some fight) *8. . . . RxPch 9. QxR RxQch 10. KxR P–Q5!,* and White resigned shortly since if the knight moves Black wins a piece with . . . QxP.

Under- and Over-Restraint

Deterring the enemy from completing his strategic plan is a typical illustration of restraint in chess. A few deft moves can often throw his pieces into confusion and gain you enough time to pursue your plan uninhibited. Missing the opportunity for restraint can doom you to wearisome defense.

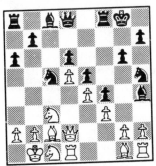

Bobotsov–Gligoric, Skopje 1972
Black to play

The first task, naturally, is to identify what the enemy plan is. Only then can you determine whether it's worth the time or piece energy to slow the enemy strategy down. In the diagram, Black can be fairly certain that White—if he does anything—will attack on the queenside. This may seem odd since his own king is on the queenside whereas the Black king is safely placed on the other side of the closed center. But White has a natural advantage in space on the queenside and this enables him to take certain liberties.

1. . . .   Q–B2?

Black's choice of a quiet, developing move turns out to be a major error. It is now that he must throw a monkey wrench into White's queenside plans—or never. With 1. . . . P–QR4 he can stop P–QN4 and force White to change plans. White could try to exploit the holes at Black QN4 and QB5 as in the game on p. 107. But Black is better prepared in this position to meet queenside threats and can turn his attention quickly to the kingside. (On p. 107 Black never got the chance.)

And what would happen on the kingside? Black would do the same thing White gets to do in the game: advance his pawns to gain space; e.g., 1. . . . P–QR4 2. N–Q3 P–N3 3. R–QB1 K–R1 4. P–QR4 P–KN4 followed by . . . R–KN1 and . . . P–N5.

2. P–QN4!   N–Q2
3. N–N3

White now has a very fine game on the queenside despite any apparent mating dangers. He will play R–QB1 and B–Q3 before opening lines with P–N5. If Black plays . . . P–QN4 now or later White can occupy the holes at QR5 and QB6 with knights. The game continued thematically.

3. . . . N–N3 4. B–Q3 N–B5 5. BxN QxB 6. N–R4 Q–B2 7. R–QB1 Q–Q1 8. N–N6 (notice how quickly White's queenside advantage becomes apparent) R–N1 9. B–B2 BxB 10. QxB N–B3 11. P–QR4 B–Q2 12. R–B3 P–N4 13. KR–QB1 B–K1 14. K–N2 N–Q2 15. P–R5 N–B3 16. N–B8! (a pretty move—threatening a deadly Q–R7) P–N3 17. NxNP B–N4 18. R–B7 N–K1 19. R–B8 RxR 20. NxR P–N5 21. N–R7 B–Q2 22. N–B6 Q–N4 23. P–N5! RPxP 24. P–R6 N–B3 25. P–R7 R–R1 26. R–B2 Q–N2 27. Q–N6 N–K1 28. N(3)–R5 *Black resigns.*

The opposite side of the coin is shown in the next example. Here White makes several errors with one move. He loses time that is needed for the kingside attack, he puts a pawn on a square where it can be captured, and he stops something that didn't need to be stopped.

Simagin–Taimanov, Moscow 1952—*1. P–QN3 P–Q4 2. B–N2 P–QB4 3. P–K3 N–QB3 4. N–KB3 N–B3 5. B–N5 B–Q2 6. 0–0 P–QR3 7. BxN BxB 8. P–Q3 P–K3 9. N–K5 R–B1 10. N–Q2 B–K2 11. P–KB4 0–0*

Position after 11. . . . 0–0

White's pieces and pawns coordinate superbly. The time has come to formulate a plan. White readily sees that there are no targets on the queenside. He can choose between action in the center (P–K4 or P–B4) and attack on the kingside (P–KN4–5 or R–B3–R3). But he has something else to consider: Black's plan.

Black has no immediately aggressive kingside play but can try to neutralize pressure there with . . . N–Q2, . . . P–KB4, and . . . B–B3. In the center Black's only thrust would be . . . P–Q5?, a move that makes his bishops inferior since White would lock the area up with P–K4. For the best chance of counterplay Black could consider . . . P–QN4 followed by . . . P–B5. This would open lines for Black's QR and at least one bishop. Therefore, Black focuses on the queenside.

| 12. P–QR4?! | B–K1 |
| 13. P–R5? | |

White focuses there also. But an examination of the position shows that . . . P–QN4 is not dangerous. White has two knights to stop . . . P–QB5, and it is hard for Black to challenge them. If White continued 12. R–B3 P–QN4 13. R–R3 B–K1 14. P–KN4 or 13. R–N3 and 14. N–N4 his attack would be very strong. White's effort to restrain—in effect to cripple—Black's queenside pawns lost time. But the damage goes beyond that.

13. . . .	**K–R1**
14. Q–K2	**N–Q2**
15. P–B4	**N–N1!**

White's QRP becomes a target long before anything of Black's. To meet the threat of . . . P–B3 and . . . N–B3xP, White must take drastic action. His kingside attack is too slow (15. R–B3 P–B3) and lacks punch now that Black can protect his KN2 and KR2 with . . . P–B3 and . . . B–N3. Moreover, White can't ignore the loss of the QRP because he has no compensating play except in the center. Thus:

16. PxP PxP 17. P–K4! P–B3 18. N(5)–B3 N–B3 19. N–R4 PxP 20. PxP N–Q5! (better than *20. . . . NxP 21. N–B5*) *21. Q–N4 Q–Q2 22. P–B5 N–B7 23. N–B4* (*23. QR–B1 N–K6*) *NxR 24. BxN R–Q1 25. N–N6 Q–Q6 26. N–Q5 RxN! 27. PxR QxQP 28. R–K1 B–Q1 29. Q–R3 K–N1 30. B–B3* (the QRP is still weak) *·QxNP 31. Q–K3 Q–Q4* and Black won.

Reducing Tension

When pieces come into conflict and when pawn exchanges are possible, a degree of tension exists on the board. This tension may benefit both players or only one of them. But once established it won't easily go away. To reduce tension by liquidating the pieces that can capture one another and/or by trading off the pawns that are in contact, you eliminate some of your options and may do away with whatever counterplay is available.

Take the following position, reached by mutually aggressive opening play *(1. P–K4 P–QB4 2. N–QB3 N–QB3 3. P–KN3 P–KN3 4. B–N2 B–N2 5. N–R3 P–K3 6. 0–0 KN-K2 7. P–Q3 0–0 8. B–K3 P–N3 9. Q–Q2 P–Q4 10. B–R6).*

Taimanov–Stein, Tiflis 1966
Position after 10. B–R6

10. . . .   P–Q5!

Black reduces the central tension with an advance rather than a capture, but the effect is similar. Prompted by the threat of a White attack on his king, Black establishes a solid center that will benefit his white-squared bishop. He can assume White will trade off Black's bad KB. Then if Black survives the kingside attack, he will have a good game positionally.

11. BxB   KxB
12. N–K2   P–K4
13. P–KB4

White needs an open line for his attack and so creates a new point of pawn tension. The advance of his KBP gives him two middlegame options—opening up the KB-file, presumably after R–B2 and QR–KB1 with BPxKP, and staging an overall pawn march with P–B5. In the current position he may be intending an immediate 14. P–B5 so that on 14. . . . P–B3 (14. . . . B–N2?? 15. P–B6ch; 14. . . . PxP 15. PxP BxP 16. RxB NxR 17. BxN) he can continue with 15. P–KN4 and break with P–KN5 or, if 15. . . . P–KN4, with 16. N–B2 and P–KR4.

13. . . .   P–B3
14. PxP??

But this is very bad. White gives up the option of P–KB5 and makes an attack along the KB-file doubtful because of Black's ability now to cover every key square (KB3 and KB2 chiefly) that may be attacked. The reduction in tension is mysterious. White had no reason to fear an exchange by Black (. . . KPxBP) because White would then recapture with his KNP and have all sorts of play later with P–B5 or P–K5.

14. . . .					**NxP**

Black gets an excellent square for his knight and prepares to find another with 15. . . . N–N5 and 16. . . . N–K6. This threat gives Black time to keep White from playing N–KB4 and thereby reduces White to his only remaining middlegame plan—opening up the queenside with P–QN4. That this is insufficient is demonstrated by:

15. N–B2 P–KN4! 16. P–QN4 PxP 17. QxP N(2)–B3 18. Q–N2 Q–Q3 19. QR–B1 B–K3 20. P–B3 QR–Q1 21. KR–Q1 R–B2 22. R–B2 PxP 23. QxBP N–Q5! 24. NxN QxN 25. QxQ RxQ 26. K–B1 P–B4! (now Black can afford to make pawn breaks because his pieces hold the initiative from here on) 27. PxP BxBP 28. K–K2 N–N5 29. R–N2 NxP 30. K–K3 R–QR5 31. B–K4 BxB 32. NxB N–N5ch 33. K–Q2 N–B7 34. NxN RxNch 35. K–B3 R–R6ch 36. R–N3 R(6)xP 37. R–N5 K–N3 38. R–Q5 R–B4 39. R–Q6ch R–B3 40. R–Q7 R–KN7 41. P–Q4 RxPch and White resigned.

In this instance White held a slight initiative in the opening but erred by cutting down the options he needed to fuel the initiative. Reducing tension is an error if you need that tension for counterplay. Also it is bad when a simplified pawn structure gives the enemy a winning plan. In the following example Black's premature resolution of the queenside tension gives White the upper hand on that side of the board. He in turn converts his queenside edge into a win when Black seeks new tension there.

Govedarica–Nemet, Yugoslavia 1977—1. P–K4 P–QB4 2. N–KB3 P–Q3 3. P–Q4 PxP 4. QxP B–Q2 5. P–B4 N–QB3 6. Q–Q2 N–B3 7. N–B3 P–KN3 8. P–QN3 B–N2 9. B–N2 0–0 10. P–KR3 Q–R4 11. B–Q3 P–QR3 12. 0–0

Position after 12. 0–0

12. . . .	P–QN4

Black realizes that if he sits and waits, White will have a choice between general queenside expansion (P–QR3 and P–QN4 followed by N–Q5) and a central push (QR–Q1, KR–K1, and N–Q5). Black's move is justified tactically by 13. PxP PxP 14. BxP NxP 15. NxN QxB or 14. NxP QxQ 15. NxQ N–QN5.

13. KR–Q1	PxP?

This may seem like a logical followup to 12. . . . P–QN4 but it severely compromises Black's game. He gains very little from the exchange of pawns, whereas White gets an excellent square for his bishop and makes his queenside pawns into an aggressive force. Instead, Black should have maintained the tension with 13. . . . KR–B1 14. QR–B1 QR–N1 with reasonable prospects. White would then have to look hard for a good way of increasing his slight edge (15. N–Q5 NxN 16. KPxN QxQ 17. RxQ N–R4 with real pressure on QB5; 15. Q–K2 N–QN5 16. B–N1 PxP; 15. P–QR3 P–N5).

14. BxP	KR–B1
15. QR–B1	B–K3
16. B–Q5!	

White maintains a sizable edge after this since a subsequent capture (16. . . . BxB 17. PxB) would drive Black's QN to a bad square. The reduction of the queenside tension also permits him to expand there (*16. . . . QR–N1 17. P–R3! Q–Q1 18. P–QN4*), and when Black later tries to create new tension it only lets White expand further *(18. . . . Q–B1 19. Q–K2 B–R3 20. R–B2 P–R4? 21. P–N5!)*.

With a won game on the queenside White is also prepared to strike in the center. That decides the game.

21. . . . N–R2 22. P–QR4 B–Q2 23. B–N3 N–R4 24. N–Q5 RxR 25. QxR R–B1 26. Q–Q3 B–N2 27. P–K5! R–B4 28. B–Q4 B–B4 29. Q–K3 P–K3 (desperation) *30. BxR PxB 31. N–N6 B–R3 32. N–N5 Q–K2 33. P–R4 P–B5 34. BxP Q–N5 35. NxKP!* and Black resigned in view of 36. R–Q8ch or 36. QxB.

Stifling Counterplay

This leads to the problems of counterplay. When your opponent has the initiative, you must find counterplay or doom yourself to passivity and waiting tactics. While passivity is not always an error, it deprives you of the activity you need to worry an opponent. Eventually he will find a winning plan and a crucial breakthrough—if you don't distract him with counterplay.

The key errors involving counterplay are *(1)* shutting off your own, *(2)* failing to stop the enemy's, and *(3)* trying to contain counterplay that can't be contained. Here is a characteristic example of a misplayed middlegame featuring counterplay errors.

Sultan Khan–Flohr, Prague 1933—*1. P–Q4 N–KB3 2. N–KB3 P–KN3 3. P–B4 B–N2 4. N–B3 P–Q3 5. P–K4 0–0 6. B–K3 QN–Q2 7. N–Q2 P–K4 8. P–Q5 N–K1 9. B–K2 P–KB4 10. P–B3*

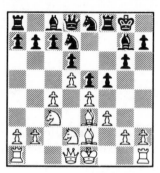

Position after 10. P–B3

Black correctly sees his best chance for piece activity on the kingside. But since White hasn't castled yet there is nothing to attack. So it is time to take stock of the various paths. One is to press on with kingside play, 10. . . . P–B5, and this is what Black selected. A better idea is to preserve the kingside options with 10. . . . N(2)–B3, possibly followed by . . . N–R4–B5. The third option is restraint on the queenside, the area White is most likely to attack. 10. . . . P–B4 is a good idea since it makes P–QN4 more difficult for White to achieve, stops P–QB5 permanently, and gives Black his own queenside chances with . . . P–QR3 and . . . P–QN4. Finally, there is the trick of 10. . . . B–R3, a positional move (intending to trade off the bad bishop) based on tactics (11. BxB Q–R5ch and 12. . . . QxB).

| **10. . . .** | **P–B5?** |

Black commits himself to one specific kingside plan, the advance of his kingside pawns with . . . P–KN4–5, possibly supported by . . . P–KR4. Here it is too slow because there is nothing yet to attack. Had he preserved his options—and counterplay—with 10. . . . QN–B3 he could meet 11. 0–0 with a now appropriate 11. . . . P–B5 (12. B–B2 P–KN4 13. R–B1 R–B2 14. P–QN4 B–B1 15. P–B5 R–N2 16. N–B4 P–N5!).

| **11. B–B2** | **P–QR4** |

Black suddenly turns to the queenside to stop White's counterplay. He has probably realized by now that his kingside assault was premature; e.g., 11. . . . P–KN4 12. P–KN4 P–KR4 13. PxP N(2)–B3 14. P–KR4 or 12. . . . PxP e.p. 13. PxP N(2)–B3 14. P–KN4 followed by N–KB1–N3–B5!.

| **12. P–QR3** | **N(1)–B3** |
| **13. P–QN4** | **P–N3?** |

Here's another error involving counterplay. Black wants to stop P–QB5, the pawn break critical to White's queenside strategy. But it is easy to see that White will be able to outgun Black for control of the key square since White can prepare P–B5 with N–N3 and R–QB1 whereas Black can only direct one more piece (. . . Q–K2) against it.

But 13. . . . P–QN3 is worse than futile. It ensures that the inevitable P–B5 will open two queenside files rather than just one because of the added pawn tension.

14. N–R4 R–K1 15. P–B5! (now 15. . . . B–B1 would give White time to play 16. BPxNP BPxNP 17. 0–0 followed by B–N5–B6, N–B4, and the addition of heavy pieces to the queenside files) *15. . . . NPxP 16. PxBP NxBP 17. NxN PxN 18. BxP N–Q2 19. B–B2 B–QR3 20. BxB RxB 21. Q–B2 R–R1 22. 0–0!* (now it's safe) *B–B1 23. KR–B1 B–Q3 24. N–B4 Q–K2 25. NxB PxN 26. QR–N1 N–B1* (26. . . . KR–B1 27. QxRch RxQ 28. RxRch K–B2 29. R–N7 also wins for White) *27. Q–B6 QR–N1 28. R–N6! RxR 29. QxR Q–Q2 30. R–B6 R–B1 31. B–K1! Black resigns.*

Poor Timing

Chess is as much a matter of timing as it is of logic, calculation, or imagination. You might conclude that N–B5 is a winning idea in a position. But that judgment may apply only to that position now. A minute ago the position was slightly different, and then N–B5 could have been a losing move. And it may be a losing move again at a later point in the game.

Haste is as much a crime as slowness, especially when making a substantial change in the status of the game. When you are about to win material or exchange queens or make a dynamic pawn break, it's worth a minute's thought to determine whether there is any rush. If your opponent can't do anything but shift a knight back and forth on the other side of the board, your game could afford an extra tempo of preparation. Your threat (or capture or pawn-break or material gain) won't run away.

Taimanov–Geller, Moscow 1955
White to move

Black has strong pressure on the QBP since he can meet 1.
P–N3 with 1. . . . P–Q4!. White appreciated the difficulty he was
getting into and played a seemingly random move:

1. P–KR4

On inspection it turns out that White has a real threat: 2. P–R5
and 3. P–R6! with great play for White's QB. How does this
threat affect Black's threat of . . . BxP? Very little. The QBP is
not going to run away. Therefore 1. . . . P–R3! would preserve
Black's advantage; e.g., 2. P–R5 N–K2 3. P–N3 P–Q4 or 3. BxN
PxB 4. Q–N4ch K–R2 5. 0–0 Q–B4ch 6. R–B2 Q–Q5 with strong
play.

1. . . .   BxP?

Black is not being greedy: he deserves that pawn. But he is
being hasty.

2. NxB	**QxN**
3. P–R5	**QxQch**
4. KxQ	**N–K2**
5. P–R6!	

Now Black has all the time in the world to meet the threat of
6. PxP KxP 7. P–KN4, but he's no longer happy. On 5. . . . N–K1
6. QR–Q1 Black becomes tied in knots. Black actually played to
simplify with 5. . . . *P–Q4* but lost eventually after 6. *RPxP KxP*
7. *PxP NxP* 8. *BxN PxB* 9. *P–KN4 KR–K1ch* 10. *K–B3 P–R3* (hop-

ing for 11. P–N5 PxP 12. PxP RxBch 13. PxR N–K5 with drawing chances) *11. QR–QB1 K–N3 12. P–B5ch K–N2 13. B–Q4 RxR 14. RxR R–K5 15. R–Q1 P–N4 16. P–N3 P–R5 17. P–N4 R–K1 18. B–N2 R–QN1 (18. . . . R–Q1 19. R–QB1) 19. RxP.*

The key element is the immediacy of threats. If you have time to take precautions, by all means take them. If the position is relatively quiet, if it is more "positional" than "tactical," if there are no tactical flashpoints between the players, you can afford to be cautious. But if the position is on the verge of becoming sharp, each tempo takes on extra value.

Spassky–Lombardy, Leningrad 1960—*1. P–K4 P–QB4 2. N–KB3 P–Q3 3. P–Q4 PxP 4. NxP N–KB3 5. N–QB3 P–QR3 6. B–KN5 QN–Q2 7. B–QB4 Q–R4 8. Q–Q2 P–K3 9. 0–0 B–K2*

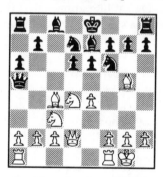

Position after 9. . . . B–K2

You couldn't say the game has been sharply played or tactical so far. It's still very early in the game. But both sides are beginning to create threats. Black, for example, has the idea of . . . P–N4–5 to win the White KP or push enemy pieces backward in defense of the pawn. He also has prospects of playing . . . P–R3! so that the bishop cannot retreat to KR4 (. . . NxKP!) or KB4 (. . . P–K4) and must go to K3 where it will be exchanged off by . . . N–N5.

White has his own tricks to work with. He can play 10. QR–Q1!, protecting his queen for instance. Then he can meet 10. . . . P–R3 11. B–R4 NxP with 12. NxN QxQ 13. RxQ BxB 14. NxPch K–K2 15. N(4)–B5ch! winning a pawn. And by protecting his queen White also prepares to answer 10. . . . 0–0 with 11. N–Q5! (11. . . . QxQ 12. NxBch and 13. RxQ). White might also select 11. QR–K1 or 11. KR–K1 with tactical play in mind.

10. P–QR3?

Although this meets the threat of . . . P–N4–N5, it wasn't immediately necessary (10. QR–Q1 P–N4 11. N–B6!). The move misuses the natural initiative White gets by making the first move of the game.

10. . . .   P–R3!

Now, since White cannot retreat to KR4 (11. B–R4 NxP 12. NxN QxQ 13. NxQ BxB), Black takes over the initiative: *11. B–K3 N–K4 12. B–R2 Q–B2 13. Q–K2* (to stop 13. . . . N–B5) *P–QN4*.

Having made one slightly wasteful and overcautious move in the opening, White now obtains a clearly inferior position by making a hasty move. Here he sees that Black cannot play 12. . . . N–B5 because of 13. QNxP! PxN 14. NxNP Q–B3 15. BxN. Therefore, White decides to take advantage of the placement of Black's centralized knight with *14. P–B4?* instead of preparing it with 15. P–R3. The difference is *14. . . . N(4)–N5*, a dangerous move because it forces the exchange of the bishop that now protects White on the weakened black squares. (White can't preserve the bishop: 15. B–Q2 Q–R2 16. Q–Q3 P–K4!).

The absence of protection on the black squares ultimately costs White the game *(15 P–R3 NxB 16. QxN 0–0 17. QR–K1 P–K4! 18. N–B5 BxN 19. PxB P–Q4*—threatening to exploit the weak squares with 20. . . . B–B4—*20. QxP B–Q3 21. Q–K2 BxP! 22. N–Q1 QR–K1 23. Q–B3 B–B4ch 24. K–R1 RxR 25. RxR Q–R4 26. N–B3 P–N5! 27. NxP QxB 28. NxNch PxN 29. Q–B6 Q–B5 White resigns)*, but it was his twin errors of overcaution and haste that brought him most of the way to defeat.

Passivity

Passivity, the practice of sitting on a position and waiting for something to happen, is justified only when you are content to draw and are worried about losing if you try to play forcefully.

The best rule of thumb is to determine the likelihood of success of your counterplay and measure it against the severity of your weaknesses. If you have good prospects of piece activity from counterplay—or if your position is so rife with exploitable weaknesses that waiting tactics are tantamount to surrender—you must try for the initiative. If your chances for taking the initiative are slim—especially if you are risking the creation of major new weaknesses to get your pieces moving—then sit tight.

Kotov–Kan, Moscow 1955
Black to move

Let's use this rule on the position above. White has a clear advantage in operating space but no obvious weaknesses to exploit. Given enough time White can prepare for a breakthrough in the center (doubling rooks on the Q-file and P–Q5) or on the queenside (doubling rooks on the QN-file followed by N–Q2–K4–B3 in preparation for P–QR4 and P–N5).

Black can choose between a waiting game, mixed with minor harassment of White's pieces, or some sort of countereffort. While a waiting game isn't necessarily fatal, here it is inferior since Black can get a good game with . . . P–QR4. For example, 1. . . . P–QR4 immediately would either force White into a premature advance—2. PxP QxP(4) 3. KR–N1 P–N3 or 2. P–N5? QxBP—or a loss of the initiative—2. KR–N1 R–R1 threatening 3. . . . PxP 4. PxP QxR.

| 1. . . . | P–QN3?! |
| 2. QR–N1 | Q–B7? |

Black apparently looked only for 2. . . . P–QB4 and decided that
3. QPxP PxP 4. P–N5 was too promising for White. But now was
the perfect time for 2. . . . P–QR4! since White would have to
relocate his forces to stop Black's efforts (3. Q–N3 QxQ 4. RxQ
PxP 5. PxP R–R1 controlling the only open file; 3. Q–B3 B–B3—
threatens 4. . . . P–B4—4. Q–B1 P–K4!).

Instead, Black brought his queen back to the center to anticipate a White breakthrough with P–Q5. But after *3. QR–B1 Q–B4
4. KR–Q1* he saw that White would make steady progress unless
arrested (4. . . . N–B3 5. N–K5 KR–Q1 6. Q–K2 P–KR3 7. B–R2
B–B1 8. R–B3 and 9. R–K3 or 9. R–B3 with prospects of kingside
attack or a return to the queenside). Stopping P–Q5 was not
enough for equality.

Belatedly, Black played *4. . . . P–QR4 5. Q–N3 PxP 6. PxP
R–R1*, and it should have been enough to keep White off balance.
Yet after *7. R–R1* Black rejected the aggressive 7. . . . B–B3
(which threatens 8. . . . RxR 9. RxR P–B4 or 8. . . . P–K4) in favor
of the passive *7. . . . N–B3?*.

After *8. N–K5* Black had to concede the open file in order to
protect his QBP and quickly went downhill: *8. . . . RxR 9. RxR
Q–K5* (9. . . . R–QB1 10. R–R7) *10. Q–QB3 R–QB1 11. K–R2
Q–K7 12. R–R7 N–K5 13. Q–R3 N–Q7 14. R–R8! RxR 15. QxRch
B–B1 16. N–Q7 P–R3 17. QxBch K–R2 18. QxP Black resigns.*

Giving Him a Winning Plan

The greatest danger of making a bid for counterplay is realized
when your opponent uses the open lines you establish to create a
winning plan. Sometimes a static position requires static play.
In merely protecting your weak points and letting your opponent
do his worst, you must be sure his worst will not be too bad. But
if the position is defensible and counterplay is scarce, don't upset
the standoff.

Steinitz–Tchigorin, Match 1892
White to move

White has a substantial edge in space and has protected his only weak point, his QRP. Yet it is not at all clear how White will make his advantage felt. With 1. B–R4, taking aim at the QBP, Black can play 1. . . . RxR 2. QxR and then "pass" with a noncommittal move like 2. . . . K–K2. If White plays 3. N–N4 Black can cover his targets with 3. . . . N–N1.

1. R–N6!

This is a fine way of maximizing White's advantage. He uses his rook on the best available square and prepares to attack the QBP with two minor pieces.

1. . . .   NxR?

In a bad position, grabbing material has a great attraction. Here, however, the exchange gives White the path to victory he needs. Without a knight Black's position cannot withstand the threat of a penetration by White pieces or the advance of the passed pawn just created. On the other hand, 1. . . . B–N2! would have put the onus back on White, who would then have to find a new winning idea without permitting . . . NxR at a later point when it might be effective.

2. BPxN

Now on 2. . . . Q–K2 3. N–K5ch K–K1 White brings his pieces to bear with 4. B–N4 Q–N2 5. B–R5ch P–N3 6. NxNP PxN 7. BxPch K–Q2 8. B–B8!, a pretty position. And on 3. . . . K–N1

White can enter a winning ending with 4. QxQ BxQ 5. NxP R–N2 6. B–K2 R–Q2 7. N–N8.

Black tried 2. . . . *Q–N2 3. N–K5ch K–N1* but was overwhelmed by *4. B–R4 Q–K2* (4. . . . B–Q2 5. Q–Q6!) *5. B–N4 Q–B3 6. Q–B3! P–R3 7. B–Q6* (7. . . . R–R1 8. QxP).

Your Attitude Is Your Error

Ask an average player why he (or she) lost their last game and the answer will probably be something like: "Well, because after 24. . . . BxR he had 25. P–B7ch" or " Because I lost a piece after 14. P–N4 RxB," and so on. In other words they see their loss in basically tactical terms and express it by citing specific moves.

While each game is different in a tactical sense, some players make the same mistakes—errors of attitude—over and over. They are addicted to a damaging state of mind when they get to a critical stage in the game, and this poisons their play. When asked to explain their loss, they see only the (tactical) trees not the overall forest. How would you as a chess pathologist explain Black's demise in this game?

D. Brown–Kramer, Philadelphia 1976—*1. P–KB3!? P–K4 2. K–B2!? B–B4ch 3. P–K3 P–Q4 4. P–KR4 P–Q5 5. B–K2 N–KB3 6. P–QR3 N–B3 7. P–QN4 B–N3 8. P–N5 N–K2 9. P–R4 P–K5 10. P–KB4 Q–Q3 11. P–KN3 N(3)–Q4 12. N–QR3 N–B4*

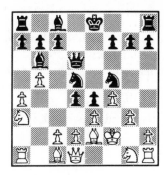

Position after 12. . . .N–B4

13. N–B4 Q–KR3 14. NxB QxN 15. P–QR5 Q–KB3 16. QR–R3 0–0 17. P–N4 N–Q3 18. K–N3 B–Q2 19. B–N2 Q–K2 20. Q–R1 N–B3 21. BxQP N(B)–K1 22. P–R5 P–KR3 23. P–B4 Q–K3 24. Q–B3 QR–B1 25. P–KB5 Q–K2 26. BxRP NxBPch 27. PxN Q–N4ch 28. K–B2 QxBPch 29. K–K1 Q–N4 30. N–R3 BxN 31. RxB Q–N7 32. B–B1 Q–N5 33. B–Q4 P–KB4 34. B–K5 P–B5 25. PxP R–B2 36. P–B5 R–B4 37. R–KN3 Q–R5 38. B–R3 *Black forfeited on time.*

You could say simply that Black lost because he failed to make the required number of moves in his alloted time. Or you could point out strategic errors (failing to restrain White with 6. . . . P–QR4 or 11. . . . P–KR4) or tactical mistakes (walking into a pin after 18. . . . B–Q2, failing to liquidate the tension with 20. . . . NxP). But one can't avoid the feeling that Black lost because he never took the game seriously.

How can you worry about a game in which your opponent's first moves are 1. P–KB3, 2. K–B2, 3. P–K3, and 4. P–KR4? One can readily imagine Black's self-assurance and his confidence that his position would win by itself. Yet White's moves, while weakening, are very difficult to exploit when the center remains closed. (The first pawn to leave the board is the QP Black lost at move 21!) Of course, White never stood well in the opening stages of the game. But Black never appreciated that his opponent still had to be beaten.

This fatal sense of security is one of several dangerous errors of attitude. Few players are objective enough to realize that the key to their failure in a particular game was something as intangible as an attitude. They would rather blame a specific move overlooked or variation miscalculated.

Besides over-optimism, the most important mistakes of attitude are trying for too much, inability to adjust to a change of fortunes, letting down, credulousness, vacillation (and its opposite, monomania), dogmatism, and drawmindedness.

Trying For Too Much

One of the important lessons of chess is very simple yet constantly forgotten: you can't get more out of a position than the position offers. If an objective analysis of the placement of pieces suggests that you have only a slight advantage, don't expect to win in a few moves. If the position is dead even, you can't avoid all the drawish continuations without risking a loss. And if you have an inferior position with little chance of successful counterattack, it doesn't pay to go all out for dynamic piece play.

Of course, if you don't even attempt an objective analysis—as Black probably didn't in the early part of the previous game—you have nothing to anchor your optimism on. Without constant evaluation of your chances, you'll always be looking for the home run when only a single is justified.

Matanovic–Petrosian, Kiev 1959—*1. P–K4 P–QB3 2. N–QB3 P–Q4 3. P–Q4 PxP 4. NxP N–Q2 5. N–KB3 KN–B3 6. NxNch NxN 7. B–QB4 B–B4 8. Q–K2 P–K3 9. B–KN5 B–K2 10. 0–0–0 B–KN5 11. P–KR3 BxN 12. QxB N–Q4 13. BxB QxB 14. KR–K1 0–0 15. K–N1 QR–Q1 16. B–N3 Q–B3*

Position after 16. . . . Q–B3

White has reason to be slightly optimistic about his chances here. It's true he has a lead in development, the more active rooks, and the advantage of a bishop over a knight. But White has no real targets and has a potential weakness of his own, his QP. To win in the middlegame would require considerable help from Black. Objectively, then, White has no reason to expect a significant advantage for many moves and should content himself to play solidly in order perhaps to win in the endgame.

17. Q–K2?!	R–Q2
18. P–QB3	P–QN4
19. P–N3	KR–Q1
20. P–KB4?	P–N5!

To avoid the drawish prospects of the endgame, White has thrown himself into a dubious adventure. Black's attack on the QP forced White's P–QB3, a move that walks into . . . P–QN4–5. Now on 21. P–B4 Black would retreat his knight to K2 or B2 with strong pressure in the center (22. Q–Q2 P–B4).

This should be a hint to White: he needs to reexamine his future prospects. If Black can force open the position around the White king, something is wrong about White's middlegame strategy. Therefore, White should conclude, it's time to bail out of the middlegame with 21. BxN! and 22. PxP, leading to a drawish ending.

21. Q–B3?	PxP
22. PxP	P–B4!

Now it is too late to secure a drawish game (23. BxN RxB 24. PxP R–N1ch! 25. K–R1 RxP puts White's king in jeopardy). In the remaining stage of the game White paid the price for his earlier overoptimism.

23. R–K5 PxP 24. BxN RxB 25. RxR PxR! 26. RxP P–KR3! 27. P–N4 (27. RxP R–N1ch 28. K–B2 Q–QN3!) *27. . . . Q–K2 28. Q–B2 R–N1ch 29. K–R1 Q–R6 30. Q–B2 R–K1 31. R–N4 P–Q5! 32. RxP R–K8ch 33. R–Q1 RxRch 34. QxR QxBPch 35. K–N1 QxP 36. P–R4 P–KR4! 37. PxP Q–B4ch 38. K–N2 QxBP 39. K–N3 Q–B4 40. K–B4 K–R2* and White sealed *41. Q–Q2* but resigned in view of Black's quickly advancing extra kingside pawns.

When you have a superior or simply more aggressive (but not necessarily superior) game, there is just as much need to evaluate rigorously.

Sydor–Gipslis, Lublin 1969—*1. P–K4 P–QB4 2. N–KB3 P–K3 3. P–Q4 PxP 4. NxP P–QR3 5. N–Q2 N–KB3 6. P–K5 N–Q4 7. B–Q3 Q–B2 8. 0–0!? QxKP 9. N–B5! Q–B2 10. R–K1 N–K2! 11. Q–B3 NxN 12. BxN N–B3 13. B–Q3 B–K2 14. N–K4 0–0 15. B–KB4 Q–Q1 16. N–Q6 P–B4*

Position after 16. . . . P–B4

White's gambit of a center pawn has given him promising compensation in terms of a temporary lead in development and a long-range restriction of Black's pieces. As long as White's knight remains on Q6, Black's queenside pieces will be spectators. And if Black plays . . . BxN, he gives White terrific play on the weakened black squares.

But the nature of White's compensation is *gradual pressure* not the opportunity of a quick knockout. With 17. QR–Q1! it's easy to see his play (17. . . . P–QN4 18. P–QB4 or 17. . . . N–N5 18. BxBP! PxB 19. Q–N3ch). But White mistakenly concludes that his compensation is so temporary—or that his opponent's confinement is so permanent—that he should play for a mate in the middlegame.

17. P–KN4?   N–N5!

White's last thrust had some good points (17. . . . PxP would permit 18. QxP R–B3 19. QR–Q1 Q–B1 20. B–N3 with strong pressure). But it is out of harmony with White's positional strengths in the center. There should be some way for Black to exploit this, and he does it by taking the initiative on the kingside. Now on 18. PxP NxB 19. QxN BxN 20. BxB RxP Black has a nice advantage with 21. . . . P–QN4, 21. . . . R–Q4, or 21. . . . Q–N3.

18. BxP

White justifies this sham sacrifice with 18. . . . PxB 19. Q–N3ch. But with P–KN4 White's kingside turns out to be weaker than Black's.

18. . . .	N–Q4!
19. B–K5!	P–KN3
20. Q–N2	B–B3!

Not 20. . . . KPxB 21. QxNch or 20. . . . NPxB 21. PxPch B–N4 22. P–KR4. Black's accurate play permits him to post a spectacular knight on KB5 and begin a powerful attack along the KB-file. The game already appears to be turning into Black's favor, and this was confirmed by:

21. B–Q3 BxB 22. RxB N–B5 23. Q–K4 Q–N3! 24. NxB (24. N–B4 N–R6ch) QRxN 25. R–KB1 QxNP 26. P–QR4 R–KB2 27. Q–K1 QR–B1 28. R–K3 Q–Q5 29. B–K4 QxP 30. BxQNP P–Q4 31. R–QN3 P–QR4 32. Q–K5 Q–B5 33. R–K1 QxP 34. QR–K3 RxB and Black won.

Change of Fortunes

Chessplayers like to think their better games have a consistent or singleminded "flow": there are no sharp changes in the initiative. The player on the attack tends to remain that way for most of the struggle.

But most games don't have this "flow." The advantage or initiative changes hands once, twice, or more. When the status quo is upset like this, both players must reevaluate their prospects and alter their attitudes to keep in tune with the position.

Kholmov–Gurgendize, Moscow 1957
Black to move

Here, for example, White has been pressing his positional advantage on the queenside for several moves. He foresees no impediment to steady progress—continuing the "flow"—in the next half dozen moves. The game continued:

1. . . .	R–R4
2. R–B2	P–R3
3. R–K2?!	Q–KN4!
4. QxBP	P–K4

But the game has taken a sharp turn as Black begins an attack on White's KR2. White was ready to meet 4. . . . Q–R5 with 5. P–KR3, but after 4. . . . P–K4 he should figure out how much danger he is in.

The position calls for concrete defensive thinking now—quite different from the optimistic positional play White was preparing a short while ago. Black can meet P–KR3 at some future point with a bishop sacrifice on KR6. How then will White defend the kingside? A tough reappraisal would show White that 5. R–Q6 is best; e.g., 5. . . . Q–R5 6. R–KN6 (attack and defense) QxPch 7. K–B2.

| 5. R–Q5? | Q–R5 |

White probably took the Black attack so lightly that he felt it could be blunted by 6. P–KR3. But that loses to 6. . . . BxP 7. R(5)xP B–B4 (7. . . . BxP 8. RxR!) 8. R–K8 and now 8. . . . Q–R8ch 9. K–B2 R–R7! 10. RxRch K–R2!! Again, we could blame this turn of events on White's failure to notice a tactical flaw (the rook sacrifice with 10. . . . K–R2). This isn't the only flaw. White is also guilty of "believing" his opponent. On 6. P–KR3 BxP 7. PxB! there is no mate and White wins. But this sloppy calculation had a broader reason: White didn't understand how serious the situation had become since the last diagram, and he didn't look hard enough.

6. R(2)xP	QxPch
7. K–B1	Q–R8ch
8. K–B2	R–R7
9. R–KN5!?	

This is desperation pure and simple. At the cost of a rook White beats off the attack and gets to threaten mate in one. Once again the attack changes hands—this time from Black to White. But this time it should be easily squelched—provided Black is mentally prepared for the new change in chances.

| 9. . . . | PxR |
| 10. RxP | RxPch?? |

But Black is unprepared. Were he to return to the defense with 10. . . . R–R2 (meeting 11. QxP mate and threatening 11. . . . Q–R5ch), White could safely resign. But influenced partly by time and pressure and partly by the momentum ("flow") of the last few moves, he looks for and plays an attacking move.

11. RxR   **Q–R5ch**

Here Black realized he had no more than a perpetual check and he agreed to a draw.

Letting Down

A similar change in attitude often occurs during a hard-fought skirmish. After several moves requiring exact calculation, boldness, and imagination, the tension is eased. The new position may require a different style of play—defensive rather than aggressive, or technical rather than speculative.

The drama is temporarily over at this point, but difficult moves remain to be found. The cardinal error is to relax. Relaxing is fine if your opponent is reduced to total passivity. But such positions rarely occur. You must remain alert.

Korchnoi–Karpov, Match 1978
Black to play

In this promising position from the world championship match, White foresees a strong central attack with P–KB4 or R–K2 and QR–K1. Both ideas prepare for P–K5, a move Black should worry about.

1. ...   **P–QB3!**

This strange move seems to open up the center for White. Yet it gives Black good counterplay once White's threats are neutralized. For the next few moves White's threats are the center of attention, and because of this, White feels himself in command of the board.

2. P–K5	BPxP
3. BxQP	QR–Q1!
4. Q–B4!	Q–B1!
5. Q–B3?!	

With this move White begins to run out of steam. He lets down slightly, perhaps thinking that he still has the upper hand.

5. . . .	PxP
6. BxKP	B–KN5!
7. QxB	QRxB
8. B–B3	KR–Q1
9. K–N2	B–Q5!

Earlier White could have anticipated all the coming trouble with 5. QR–Q1. He appears to be still waiting for something to happen on the kingside, where he once held prospects of attack.

10. QR–B1	P–KN3
11. Q–K2?	

After this White is headed for a loss. Again he could have anticipated danger with 11. KR–Q1, which forces a series of exchanges that should ensure a draw. After *11. . . . Q–Q3!* Black monopolized the Q-file with heavy pieces and eventually forced a winning endgame with *12. BxB RxB 13. Q–N5?! R–QN5 14. R–K8ch K–N2 15. RxR QxR 16. Q–K2 Q–Q4ch.* White never revived from his middlegame, postcrisis letdown.

A more spectacular example of the Letdown spoiled one of the brilliancies of the turn of the century. In this case the fault can't be placed on White's failure to reassess the position after the initial fireworks were over. He correctly continued at that point to play for a win. The fault was White's failure to look for more fireworks.

Janowski–Pillsbury, Nuremberg 1896—*1. P–K4 P–K4 2. N–KB3 N–QB3 3. B–N5 N–B3 4. 0–0 NxP 5. R–K1 N–Q3 6. NxP B–K2*

7. B–Q3 N–N5? 8. B–B1 0–0 9. N–QB3 N–B4 10. P–QR3 N–B3
11. N–Q5 B–B4 12. N–Q3 B–Q3 13. Q–N4 KN–Q5 14. P–QN4!
P–B4 15. Q–R5!! NxBP 16. B–N2 NxQR 17. BxN N–K2 18.
N(3)–B4 P–B3 19. RxN! QxR (19. . . . BxR 20. B–B4!) 20. NxQch
BxN

Position after 20. . . . BxN

White has a substantial material advantage thanks to an
imaginative attack, and it takes several second- and third-best
moves to permit Black to draw. Often the Letdown comes when
a player fails to crown his tactical success with technical or
strategic accuracy. Here White relaxes in a different way. He
begins by failing to find the tactical win with 21. B–B4ch P–Q4
(21. . . . K–R1 22. N–N6 mate) 22. NxP PxN 23. BxPch K–R1 24.
B–B7! followed by B–N6.

The game proceeded: *21. Q–R3? P–Q4 22. N–R5 P–KN3 23.
Q–QB3 K–B2! 24. Q–N7ch K–K1.* White got a second chance to
deliver the tactical coup de grâce, this time with 25. B–B6!; e.g.,
25. . . . R–B2 26. Q–N8ch R–B1 27. N–N7ch K–Q1 28. QxRch
or 25. . . . B–Q3 26. B–K2! followed by scooping up the kingside pawns with his queen.

White chose another forcing line, *25. N–B6ch? BxN 26. BxB,*
but after *26. . . . R–B2 27. Q–N8ch R–B1* he could escape a repetition of moves (Black's rook constantly attacking White's queen
as it shifts from KN7 to KN8) with *28. QxRP RxB.* It took a few
more errors by White, but eventually the game ended with a
handshake.

"Believing Him"

A virtual prerequisite to effective calculation is a degree of confidence in your own ability. Say you count out a sequence and come to the conclusion that the final position is in your favor. You can still undo all this mental effort by second-guessing yourself and playing a different line because you don't trust your own mind. Even the most hard-headed of players are guilty of this fault from time to time.

But there is something worse than excessively questioning your own play—not questioning your opponent's. "Nobody bluffs in chess," you might assume. "Therefore, there must be a reason for that last move of his. It looks bad, but he must have something there." So you end up believing him and disdaining the effort to refute his last move. (Usually you find out painfully in the post-mortem analysis how wrong you were. "What would you have done if I had played . . . ?" you ask, only to discover that his own analysis was all wrong and that your line of play would have put the game out of reach.)

Saidy–Commons, Eagle Rock 1974
Black to move

In this situation White's king is a bit uncomfortable but very hard to embarrass. Actually it is quite safe around the center pawn phalanx, and White's other pieces have just as much opportunity as Black's. For example, 1. . . . R–B3 2. Q–Q7 R(1)–KB1 can be met effectively by 3. R–N7. Meanwhile, White is preparing to play R–N7, P–B4, or R–QR1.

For no other reason than desperation and a mutual shortage of time, Black played:

1. . . .   **RxP!??**

Black might be bluffing. Or he could have miscalculated. Or he might simply be trying the best practical chance in a lost position. White can't be sure what is behind 1. . . . RxP. But he should make the effort. Had he done so, he surely would have seized the rook and won since 2. KxR! QxP, for example, can be met by 3. R–N8, 3. P–Q4, 3. N–N6ch K–R2 4. K–N3, or some other safe line. But White had more faith in his opponent than in his own position or his own calculations.

2. P–B4??   **R–B3**

And now White is really in trouble. There might follow 3. Q–B7 RxNch 4. QxR R–K3, for example. The game actually went 3. *Q–B7 RxNch 4. K–Q4 RxKP 5. R–N8ch K–R2 6. R–KN1 R–KN7 7. RxR QxR 8. PxB PxP*, but the future was already certain. Black won.

For another case, take Landau–Ozols, Kemeri 1937, which began with 1. *P–Q4 N–KB3 2. P–QB4 P–K3 3. N–QB3 B–N5 4. P–K3 P–B4 5. KN–K2 N–B3 6. P–QR3 BxNch 7. NxB PxP 8. PxP P–Q4 9. P–B5 0–0 10. B–K2 P–K4! 11. PxP NxP 12. B–KN5? P–Q5! 13. N–K4 Q–Q4! 14. NxNch? PxN 15. BxP QxNP 16. QxP.* White's last move is the most dangerous try in a rapidly declining position. But is the sacrifice of two rooks sound?

Black evidently thought so. His next move was a double mistake. The first and most important error was failing to grab while the grabbing was good: 16. . . . QxRch! 17. K–Q2 QxR, and Black would prosper after 18. QxN Q–KN8! (meeting the 19. Q–N5 mate threat) 19. B–Q3 QxPch 20. K–B3 P–KR3 (meeting the 21. BxPch KxB 22. Q–R5ch threat) 21. B–R8 Q–N7. Even a neutral defensive move like 16. . . . N–N3 would have been a very bad mistake. But it was doubly bad because the move chosen, *16. . . . N–B3??,* walked into a favorable liquidation: *17. Q–Q5! Q–N3* (17. . . . QxQ 18. R–N1ch mates) *18. Q–N5,* and White won because of his extra pawn and Black's weakened kingside.

Finally, there is an even more embarrassing kind of error. Instead of believing their opponent (and not trusting themselves) players believe third parties. I've known players to resign in drawable positions or offer draws in superior games because of the looks on the faces of spectators watching their games(!). And this remarkable position once decided a British woman's championship.

Black to move

Black sealed *1. . . . Q–B4ch* and prepared to see at her home analysis board whether there was any hope of a win. But the spectators scoffed at this, thinking that the position was dead drawn. The weight of authority in favor of a draw was too much for Black, who agreed to a half point without continuing.

Yet the position is dead *won: 2. K–R6 Q–R6ch 3. K–N7 Q–N5ch 4. K–R6 Q–R5ch 5. K–N7 Q–N4ch 6. K–R7 K–B2!*, and Black must move her queen away permitting a mate. Moral: Trust yourself.

Vacillation and Monomania

Anyone who, as a child, was confused by contradictory maxims ("Haste makes waste" and "Look before you leap" versus "He who hesitates is lost") would be equally baffled by many bits of chess advice. For every rule, admonition, and guideline there seems to be a contrary rule. For every evil to be avoided there is an opposite evil.

Don't grab pawns says one authoritative adage. But don't pass up free material says another. Counterplay is vital, according to one bit of advice. But breaking out of passivity to gain counterplay is frequently folly. And so on.

In terms of the logical order of chess thought there is another twin set of dangers; monomania—concentrating on one idea to the detriment of others—and vacillation—straying back and forth from one plan to another. We've already said that you must recognize changes in fortune and alter your plans and tactical ideas. But mindless changes in planning, attitude, or tactics are also fatal.

An example of monomania is the Magnificent Obsession. Often a grand idea takes hold of a player's imagination as if it had burrowed into the brain like a gopher. Nothing will root it out. You might convince yourself that a particular line of tactical play fails at this moment. But for the rest of the game it keeps popping up in your thoughts. Mikhail Tal blamed such a monomaniacal gopher for his loss to Alexei Suetin in the 1977 tournament at the Black Sea resort of Sochi (It began with *1. P–K4 P–K4 2. N–KB3 N–KB3 3. NxP P–Q3 4. N–KB3 NxP 5. P–Q4 P–Q4 6. B–Q3 B–K2 7. 0–0 N–QB3 8. P–B4 N–B3 9. N–B3 0–0 10. R–K1 PxP 11. BxP B–KN5 12. B–K3 N–QR4 13. B–Q3 R–K1 14. P–KR3 B–R4 15. P–R3 P–QR3 16. P–Q5 P–B4! 17, B–KN5 P–N4.*)

Position after 17. . . . P–N4

"Farther back I had thought that 17. . . . P–N4 was impossible," Tal explained, "and I was all set to play 18. P–Q6 QxP 19. BxN, and now Black would lose if he captured with either the queen (19. . . . QxB 20. N–Q5 Q–Q3 21. NxBch RxN 22. BxPch! KxB 23. QxQ) or the bishop (19. . . . BxB 20. BxPch).

"But after 19. . . . PxB! I would have nothing to show. For about forty minutes I twisted this position around in my mind and tried 19. N–K4 (after 18. P–Q6 QxP), but nothing came of that either."

Meanwhile White's time was being exhausted, and he had to come to terms with the attack on his QP. Tal continued his search for a tactical method of advancing the pawn.

18. R–K5	**B–N3**
19. BxB	

"The planned advance of the QP was an obsession, and instead of continuing 19. N–KR4 White sacrificed a pawn," Tal recalled. The variations might have run something like 19. N–KR4 BxB 20. QxB N–B5 21. R–K2 NxQP 22. QR–K1! N–B5! 23. QxQ NxRch 24. RxN QRxQ 25. BxB R–Q7 with a roughly balanced ending. Tal wanted more.

19. . . .	**RPxB**
20. P–Q6?	**QxP**

Not 20. . . . BxP 21. RxRch winning a piece. Tal's idea behind P–Q6 was to create a pin on the K-file. But if he had played the immediate 20. Q–K2 Black could have liquidated the pressure with 20. . . . B–Q3 and stood well.

21. Q–K2	**N–B5!**
22. N–K4	**Q–Q1**
23. R–Q1	**NxR!**

This permits Black to demonstrate why two rooks are often superior to a queen: *24. RxQ NxNch 25. QxN QRxR 26. BxN BxB 27. NxBch PxN 28. QxP R–Q7! 29. QxRP RxNP 30. Q–QB6 R–K8ch 31. K–R2 R(K)–K7 32. P–N4 (or 32. QxBP RxP 33. Q–Q5 RxPch with a won king-and-pawn ending) 32. . . . P–B5 33. K–N3 R–N6ch 34. K–R4 RxBP 35. K–N5 RxKRP 36. P–R4 P–B6! (the last trap was 36. . . . PxP 37. Q–K8ch K–N2 38. QxPch! with a stalemate) 37. PxP P–B7 and White resigned.*

The computers are the only chessplayers who don't have to worry about monomania. Every time a chess-programmed machine looks at a position it is as if it were the first time. The pieces have no memories—and neither does the computer that moves them. The "thoughts" a machine was weighing when considering its last move are now ancient history. One result can be vacillation.

White to move

This position, cited by David Levy in his excellent work, *Chess and Computers*, illustrates the hazard of spontaneous thought. It occurred in a computers-only event, and the program playing White was obviously winning. White could have mated in one move with either 1. B–B4 or 1. Q–N2. Or he ("it") could have mated in two moves with any number of noncommittal first moves. But this particular program could not place a higher value on a one-move mate than on a two-move mate. All mates were created equal, it thought. So:

1. K–B1?

This is no worse than any other move (aside from 1. B–B4 or 1. Q–N2 mate) since White retains the possibility of mate next move.

1. ....   **P–KB4**
2. K–B2?

Again, not a bad move in the sense that mate is still available next time around. But you can already get the picture. Play continued:

2. . . .	**P–B5**
3. K–B1?	**P–N5**
4. K–B2?	**P–B6**
5. K–B1	**PxP**
6. K–B2??	**PxR=Q**
7. K–B1???	

Each time the computer played a king move it had "forgotten" the available mate and had chosen a neutral move which preserved a mate on the following move. (This was just as good as an immediate mate in this computer's thinking.) But here it makes an incredible error, overlooking a check.

7. . . .	**QxBch**

And Black eventually won.

Humans show a different set of vacillation problems. They might seem to forget their previous moves and thinking when considering a tactical idea.

Polugaevsky–Averbakh, Moscow 1956
White to move

White has a spirited attack brewing but he must be careful. On 1. BxP?? for example, Black wins with 1. . . . R–B7!. White found an ingenious winning alternative.

1. P–B6!

Now on 1. . . . R–B7 White wins with 2. P–B7ch. Furthermore, he can meet 1. . . . PxP with 2. N–B5; e.g., 2. . . . R–B7 3. RxB RxB 4. Q–N3ch or 2. . . . R–KN5 3. RxB RxR 4. QxRch QxQ 5. N–K7ch.

1. . . .	NxP
2. BxP??	

It's as if White, like the computer, never saw this position or a similar one before. The thinking behind 1. P–B6 *had* to be the evacuation of KB5 for a knight. White would have capped a neat victory had he continued 2. N–B5; for example, *(a)* 2. . . . Q–Q2 3. BxP R–B7 4. RxB NxN 5. N–R6ch! PxN 6. Q–N3ch; *(b)* 2. . . . R–B7 3. Q–N3 (so that 3. . . . RxPch 4. QxR BxQ is met by 5. RxQch) 3. . . . R–B2 4. BxP R–Q2 5. BxN QxB 6. N–R6ch! QxN 7. Q–N8ch; or *(c)* 2. . . . R–KN5 3. N–K3!! R–Q5! 4. NxB R(Q)xN 5. B–R3 R–R4 6. B–N4 (analysis by Aronin).

White might not have foreseen all these possibilities when he played 1. P–B6, but surely he must have planned to play 2. N–B5 when he pushed the KBP. What happens now is hideous.

2. . . .	R–B7!

The only difference between this position and the one follow-ing 1. BxP R–B7 in the last diagram is White's opportunity to play 3. BxN here, hoping for 3. . . . PxB 4. N–K4!. But Black was awake.

3. BxN RxPch 4. K–R1 R–Q7ch! (so that White can't capture the bishop with a rook or play 5. K–N1 BxQ 6. BxQ BxR) *5. N–K4 RxR 6. RxR Q–K1! 7. Q–N3 QxNch 8. K–R1 Q–R8ch,* and White conceded in view of 9. K–B2 R–B7ch 10. K–K3 Q–K5 mate.

This was tactical vacillation. Strategic vacillation is no better. It may not be punished as quickly but it costs vital time..

Schmidt–Mariotti, Nice 1974
White to move

White has a pleasant position in view of his opponent's lag-gard development and bad bishop. But such advantages are difficult to exploit in a blocked position. White must choose a plan.

It isn't as easy as it looks. He could try 1. P–B5 and force open the queenside with P–QR3 and P–QN4xP or P–QN4–5xP. The drawback to this plan is Black's ability to play . . . P–K4 quickly, freeing his game. White would still have a good game, but per-haps 1. P–QR3 and 2. P–QN4 is better preparation for P–B5 since Black would not enjoy the defense of an isolated QP after 1. . . . P–K4 2. QPxKP followed by BPxQP. Or perhaps 1. P–K3, a good waiting move that takes the sting out of . . . P–KB5, is best. Then White can decide on a plan next move.

> **1. QR–Q1?** **P–QN3**
> **2. Q–Q2?!**

But there is no logic behind this essentially defensive group-ing of White's pieces. After 1. . . . P–QN3 it was time to choose a plan such as 2. PxP BPxP 3. Q–B7! and 4. R–QB1, admitting that 1. QR–Q1 was silly.

> **2. . . .** **B–R3**
> **3. R–B1**

Now it becomes apparent that White can't decide on a plan, perhaps thinking that the closed center gives him the luxury of lingering over a choice. He seems to have abandoned whatever action he planned with 1. QR–Q1 and 2. Q–Q2 (could it have been preparation for P–KB3 and P–K4?) and now plans to open the QB-file with BPxP.

| 3. ... | QR–B1 |
| 4. P–B5? | |

And finally White commits himself, but to a bad plan at this point. With 4. Q–K3 and N–B4 he would still have a quite reasonable, but no longer so favorable, game. Or he could continue 4. PxP and exchange rooks on the QB-file to enable White's pieces to penetrate in the ending. That, at least, would be consistent with his last move, although not with his first two.

4. ...	BxN
5. PxB	PxP
6. PxP	

White's idea was to isolate the Black QRP and develop strong pressure (as after 6. ... NxP 7. N–Q4, for instance).

| 6. ... | P–K4! |
| 7. KR–K1? | |

A final error. The only consistent move was 7. QxP, but that would give Black a strong queenside initiative after 7. ... R–R1 8. Q–Q2 R–R6! followed by ... KR–R1 or ... R–N1–N4. Having forsaken consistency earlier, White remains erratic:

7. ... Q–Q1 8. R–K2 P–N3 9. P–KR4 (trying for kingside action of all things with B–R3 and P–KN4) R–N1 10. B–R3 R–N5! 11. N–N5 NxN 12. PxN P–K5! 13. PxP N–K4! 14. Q–B3 P–Q5 15. Q–R1 N–B6ch 16. K–N2 NxP! 17. R–Q1 NxB 18. P–R3 P–B5! 19. KxN (19. PxR P–B6ch 20. K–R2 PxR 21. RxP QxR!) 19. ... Q–N4 *and White resigned.*

Dogmatism

Most of the common errors played today can be described as violations of basic principles. These principles, discovered by trial and error and then formulated by the great masters at the end of the last century, separate the haphazard chess of the 1870s from the more purposeful plan of the 1970s. At least the players of today should know better when they do something like delay development or cripple their pawns.

But adherence to these general principles can be an error of a different kind, the error of dogmatism. General principles are precisely that—general. They can't apply to all cases. The only way to be sure that the general principles should be adhered to in a particular game is to analyze concrete variations. If you discover that the natural move in a given position is bad, look for antipositional moves and subject them to the same analysis.

Euwe–Keres, Match 1939–40
White to move

Where should White move his attacked knight? The natural moves are *(a)* to direct it toward the center, N–K5; *(b)* to eliminate the obnoxious Black knight, N–Q2; or *(c)* to defend the key squares around the king, N–K1. But each of these moves poses new problems, as analysis reveals.

On 1. N–K5, for example, Black plays 1. . . . NxB 2. RPxN B–B4! and the threat of 3. . . . P–B3 is too strong. Here it seems ironic that moving the attacked piece to the center puts it on one of the few squares on which it can be trapped. Also, on 1. N–Q2 White walks into a pin with 1. . . . R–Q1 2. R–B2 B–B4 3. B–R4 R–Q2 (after which Black has the diabolical threat of 4. . . . P–N6! 5. BxP NxB 6. RPxN BxRch or 5. BPxP N–B7ch). Finally, on 1. N–K1 Black can give an embarrassing rook check on the Q-file and follow with 2. . . . R–Q7ch.

White's choice, then, is limited to the unnatural moves, 1. N–N1 and 1. N–R4. In the game, White chose the former, perhaps because putting the knight on KR4 looked silly. There is a general principle ("A knight on the rim brings shame," as a German aphorism puts it) warning against such decentralization. Besides, the knight is stalemated on KR4.

Yet after 1. N–R4 Black has no decisive stroke, since 1. . . . R–Q1ch 2. K–K1 R–Q7 can be met by 3. P–B3!, removing the defender on K4. Concrete analysis would have shown White why 1. N–N1 was bad—1. . . . R–Q1ch 2. K–K1 R–Q7 3. P–B3 RxKNP! (4. PxN RxNch or 4. K–B1 PxP). That's what happened in the game, and White lost.

Drawmindedness

To most beginning chessplayers, a draw is a relatively rare result. Their games are usually decided by bad moves—often very bad moves—which make losing inevitable for the guilty party. But the improving player learns to reduce the frequency of his outright blunders and discovers that sometimes, despite all his ingenuity, good moves alone cannot force a victory. The result is a draw. All winning chances are exhausted.

At the higher ranks of chess, the most common result of a game is, in fact, a draw. The masters have a better idea of what it takes to lose a game, and their avoidance of the losing errors keeps the position within the "draw radius."

But the player who is eager to draw is frequently surprised at how difficult a split point is to achieve. This is because there are few automatic methods of forcing a draw. One is to reduce the board's material to nothingness. Another is to check the enemy king perpetually. But otherwise you have to work hard to draw.

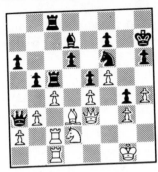

Sarapu–Gipslis, Sousse 1967
White to move

White is the player eager to shake hands in this position. Black has considerable queenside pressure and—despite the apparent weakness of his kingside—faces nothing in the way of serious counterplay. It's not certain how Black will be able to make progress, however. White prepares for a possible liquidation of forces into an ending.

1. K–B2!?	K–N2
2. K–K2	P–QR4

With this advance Black announces his intention to play . . . P–R5. Even at the optimum moment this break would promise only slim chances of a win since White has an excellent defensive position, however passive it may be. Moreover, White can liquidate the heavy pieces immediately with 3. PxP! RxR 4. RxR RxR 5. BxR BxPch 6. B–Q3 or 5. . . . QxRP 6. B–Q3.

3. N–N1?	Q–N5
4. P–R3??	

White wants a draw so badly that he rushes into a combination that he thinks will lead to a perpetual attack on the enemy queen. The drawing idea has a small hole: White overlooks an escape square and as a result his position dissolves.

But it would be wrong simply to blame his calculation. His biggest mistake was one of misjudgment. Rather than play the natural drawing idea of 3. PxP—which is not an automatic draw and requires hard work—he jumped at the easy way out. (Note that now 4. PxP is not so good as before—4. . . . RxR 5. RxR RxR 6. BxR BxPch 7. B–Q3 NxP or 7. K–B2 B–B3—but still improves on White's 4. P–R3.)

4. . . .	QxNP
5. R–B3	Q–N7ch
6. R(1)–B2	Q–R8!

White had counted on 6. . . . QxN 7. R–B1 Q–N7ch 8. R(1)–B2 Q–R8 9. R–B1 with a perpetual attack on the queen. After 6. . . . Q–R8! White played 7. N–Q2 PxP 8. NxP Q–R8! 9. R–B1, and after 9. . . . Q–N7ch he resigned.

Another drawing method with a strong appeal is to seal up the board to prevent a breakthrough. It works only when there is absolutely no open line available for enemy breakthrough or when you can control the few open lines that are available.

This method of drawing can be infuriating to the opponent. For example, in one grandmaster game—Kavalek–Bronstein, Amsterdam 1968—Black's pawn fortress after twenty-five moves was so solid that it drove White to an unsound sacrifice. (The game went *1. P–K4 P–K3 2. P–Q4 P–Q4 3. N–QB3 B–N5 4. P–K5 P–QN3 5. P–QR3 B–B1 6. P–B4 N–K2 7. N–B3 Q–Q2 8. B–K3 QN–B3 9. B–B2 B–N2 10. B–Q3 0–0–0 11. P–QN4 P–B3 12. N–K2 K–N1 13. P–B3 P–KR3 14. P–KR4 P–KR4 15. N–B1 N–B4 16. N–N3 N–R3 17. P–R4 N–N5 18. P–R5 N–K2 19. Q–Q2 N–B1 20. 0–0 P–KB4 21. KR–N1 P–QN4! 22. P–R6 B–B3 23. N–B5 Q–K1 24. N–N5 B–Q2 25. R–R5 P–B3 26. P–B4? QPxP 27. BxQBP PxB 28. N–N7 NxB 29. QxN B–K2 30. P–N5 PxP 31. NxP BxP! 32. QxB BxN 33. NxR QxN 34. QRxPch N–N3 35. QxQch RxQ 36. RxNch PxR 37. RxPch K–R2 38. RxB R–QB1! 39. R–K7ch KxP 40. R–K6ch K–N4 White resigns.*)

But it usually takes the skills of a grandmaster to foresee how solid such a pawn fortress will be. For lesser mortals—and even for grandmasters in some positions—the way to the draw is much harder.

Chekhover–Capablanca, Moscow 1935
White to move

White's greatest error in this game was his lack of ambition. He is, in fact, slightly better situated than his opponent. His advantage is not large enough to justify anything violent (1. P–K5? PxP 2. PxP N–N5 only weakens the KP). But with judicious regrouping (1. P–N3 and 2. Q–N2 or Q–B1) White will be ready to build a breakthrough in the center or on the queenside.

1. P–Q5?	**P–K4**

White knew that Black would play 1. . . . P–K4 because the other moves would only enlarge White's small edge (1. . . . PxP 2. KPxP gives White a good file and anything else permits 2. PxP PxP 3. P–K5!). White has thus closed the center at the cost of worsening his bishop and denying himself the breakthrough he needs in the center. His drawish intentions were evident from the next several moves.

2. P–N3	**N–B1**
3. Q–B1	**B–B1**
4. P–KR3	**P–R3**

Black positions his pieces and pawn for a kingside break (. . . K–R2, . . . N–N1, . . . P–N3, and . . . P–B4). With the center closed, he can take his time with preparatory moves. White, having committed himself earlier, now sees that his counterplay possibilities (P–QR3 and P–QN4/P–KB4) are few.

5. N–R4	P–KN4
6. N–B5	BxN
7. PxB	Q–Q2
8. P–KN4?!	K–N2
9. P–QR4?	

With this cementing of the queenside, White has nearly completed his pawn fortress. But as long as there is one possible point of breakthrough, he is in trouble. That breakthrough will come along the KR-file, and it is impossible for White to stop it. For this reason, White should have retained the glimmer of queenside counterplay contained in P–QR3 and P–N4.

This didn't necessarily doom White—it only made his defensive task unrelievedly tedious. The game proceeded with great maneuvering and preparation.

9. . . . *N(1)–R2 10. P–B3 R–KR1 11. K–B2 QR–KN1 12. R–R1 P–R4 13. QR–K1 K–B1 14. Q–B2 K–K2 15. Q–N2 Q–Q1 16. N–N5 Q–N1 17. Q–R1 N–Q2 18. Q–B1 N(Q)–B3 19. Q–R1 K–Q2 20. N–B3 K–B1 21. R–K2 N–B1 22. R(2)–K1 N(1)–Q2 23. Q–N1 K–N2*

Black still has a long way to go since whenever he plays . . . PxP White will recapture with the BP and deny him an open file. Therefore Black must prepare further so that after the exchange of pawns he can break through with . . . P–K5 or with a sacrifice on KR6.

However, White eased his task immeasurably with his next-to-last error, *24. N–K4?*. This was bad because after *24. . . . NxN* he couldn't avoid a serious line-opening (25. RxN N–B3 26. R–K2 P–K5! 27. BPxP PxP). That led to the finale.

25. PxN N–B3 26. B–B3 R–N2 27. R(K)–N1 Q–N1 28. Q–QB1 K–B2 29. Q–K3 PxP 30. PxP R(2)–R2 31. Q–B1 R–R5 32. RxR RxR 33. R–N2 Q–N2! 34. K–K2 Q–R3 35. K–Q3 R–R8 36. Q–Q2 Q–R6 37. Q–K2 R–QN8, and after 38. K–B3? R–K8! White resigned (39. QxR QxBch or 39. Q–Q3 RxP! wins decisive material).

Practical Mistakes

People make mistakes when faced with choices. So far we've considered mistakes made out of poor attitudes, misunderstanding or ignorance of the game's basic elements (tactical, positional, and strategic), and sloppy thinking. But there is another, albeit ill-defined, category of error that goes to the heart of the choosing process.

These practical mistakes occur because of a breakdown in the process. The breakdown may occur because of a faulty vision—what some players magnify by calling a "hallucination." They see things (on the board) that aren't there. Or they don't see things they should.

Or they are hypnotized by attractive but second-best moves. They get fancy. They overfinesse. They despair. For whatever reason, they don't look for the best move.

"Hallucination"

The most bizarre form of visual error occurs when you seemingly forget how the pieces move. This isn't supposed to happen to experienced players, you say? Only to beginners?

Grinfeld–Pankina, Kirov 1974
White to move

This example, from a high-level team tournament, is a fine specimen of hallucination. White is two pawns ahead and enjoys good winning chances.

1. Q–N3ch???	**KxQ**

And White, who suddenly realized that the pawn on KR4 did not protect the queen, was forced to resign. A chess nightmare.

Such mistakes are relatively rare. But even the best players occasionally make comparable errors in their mind when looking a few moves ahead. Consider the misfortune of young Mikhail Tal, several years before he became world champion.

Tal was already a strong player at the time and was playing his first match against a master. He fended off a brutal attack in one critical game and was ready to consolidate a material advantage into victory. But suddenly he calculated a beautiful winning idea. Both kings came under attack and every tempo was vital. Then, Tal recalled, "I discovered that the whole point of my combination lay in the move Bishop (from KB8) to KN5."

The move was, of course, impossible, and Tal lost. Somewhere in his calculations he had "moved" the bishop mentally to KR6 or K7, permitting it to land on KN5 at the decisive moment.

These errors are the easiest to explain and hardest to anticipate of all the blunders you can make. When you begin to play chess you are concerned about the capabilities of the pieces, e.g., "Can he take me if I play Q–B4?" But as you progress in playing ability, your concern turns to more sophisticated levels. When evaluating a move you measure it against a foundation of dos and don'ts—"Don't weaken your pawns without reason," for instance.

But you abandon the early warning system that ensures against visual errors as you mature in chess skill. The warning system becomes unwieldy. If Tal had stopped at each point in his thought process and asked, "Can my rook really move three squares laterally?", "Is my bishop able to go to KN5?", the interruption would stifle his thinking. In order to calculate a single move ahead the thought process must be smoother and more automatic.

These instances of hallucination or chess blindness are more than oversights. Good players have been known to shift their bishops from white squares to black ones during calculation. Yefim Geller, the prominent Soviet grandmaster, once lost to Bobby Fischer because in a critical variation he calculated the capture of a rook by a king that was four squares away. And Geller was the beneficiary of another hallucination:

Boleslavsky–Geller, Zurich 1953
White to move

White played *1. P–R3*, preparing a blunder. He had seen *1. . . . PxPch 2. KxP NxBP! 3. NxN R–B6ch* coming. He realized that his king and knight would be under double attack. But he thought he could play 4. R–Q3(!) protecting both attacked pieces.

Since 4. R–Q3 is quite illegal, White was forced to move his king. Eventually he was smothered under an avalanche of Black pawns on the kingside.

It's a Big Board

No one can concentrate on sixty-four squares at once. We focus on one theater of action—perhaps ten to fifteen squares in size—and then on another. Usually we don't have to worry about the rest of the board since queenside pieces tend to have little impact on the kingside. And that's how we forget about the rest of the board. Our horizon is framed in our mind. We simply don't see pieces beyond the horizon.

Reshevsky–Savon, Petropolis 1973
White to move

With more time White surely would have found the forced mate with 1. R–R8ch K–N4 2. P–R4ch KxP 3. RxPch PxR 4. QxP or some other winning line. But he didn't have enough time and got careless.

1. QxPch???   **BxQ**
White resigns

White was committing a second error (failing to look carefully when you are about to play what seems to be the decisive move). But his horrible blunder was mainly due to the horizon effect. The bishop had moved down to QN8 six moves before. White had just forgotten about it.

Even with plenty of time, as in a skittles game or in a typical middlegame position in tournament chess, pieces suddenly become lost. You can forget about them remarkably quickly. A piece may be part of the action in a particular sector, pass out of con-

sideration since it goes off into a second sector, and then emerge
with humiliating impact in a third, and vital, sector.

Hecht–Polugaevsky, Belgrade 1970
White to move

White had had a murderous attack for several moves before
the diagramed position was reached. Now he looks for the killer.
There may be a mate with 26. BxP PxB 27. RxP and 28. Q–R2,
but White wasn't convinced. Instead, he toyed with the idea of
checking the Black king into the corner at KR1. If he could do
that, then RxPch!/ . . . PxR/ P–N7ch would win out of hand. So,
he found this sequence:

| **1. N–B6** | **BxB** |

On 1. . . . BxN 2. BxB QxB White accomplishes his goal with
3. QxPch K–R1 4. RxPch! PxR 5. P–N7ch K–R2 6. PxR(N)ch!.
Brilliant.

| **2. N–K7ch** | **K–R1** |
| **3. RxPch** | |

Everything appears to have worked out for White . . .

| **3. . . .** | **BxR!** |

. . . with the exception of the bishop that wasn't supposed to
reappear on the kingside.

There is no insurance against visual errors like these, but some
safeguards offer protection. The first safeguard is to recheck
calculated sequences in your mind before you play them. At the

critical point in the sequence ask yourself, "Where are my pieces and where are his?" In the above example White could have saved himself an embarrassing surprise by searching his mind for the location of Black's black-squared bishop when he prepared for 3. RxPch.

A second safeguard, proposed for tournament play by Donald Byrne, is also a good cure for missed opportunities (p. 191). Byrne suggested getting a different perspective by arising from the board and concentrating on the position mentally. This remarkable method sometimes permits you to "see" things with your mind that you didn't with your eyes. When you look directly at the board you may mentally block out certain possibilities. Away from the board, you can all of a sudden realize, "Oh, my bishop is threatening a fork at Q6." Surprisingly, this exercise has helped many players of all playing strengths.

Pretty Moves

One of the great joys of chess is playing beautiful moves, moves that put material en prise, defy general principles and logic, or simply create remarkable positions. But there is a greater joy for many players: winning.

You don't have to forsake pretty moves to win, as many of these games show. But the highest priority in choosing a move must be its usefulness to you. Art in a museum doesn't have to do anything. But artistic chess moves must pass a test of utility.

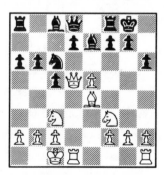

Scott–Sanchez, Phoenix 1978
White to move

Here White has achieved a powerfully centralized position against a much stronger opponent. (Black was rated 700 points above White according to the Elo rating system, meaning that he should win nearly every game the two players have with each other.) White now looks for a way to exploit his great control of the board's center.

1. B–N6?

It's not often a weaker player gets to tease an opponent with such a move. The bishop cannot be taken, of course, nor can the Black king move out of the pin (1. . . . K–R1 2. BxP). But the trouble with 1. B–N6 is that it's value is entirely pictorial. The move simply doesn't accomplish anything. There is no way White can bring additional pressure to bear on KB7.

A much better, although less spectacular, way of continuing was the preparatory 1. P–QR3 and 2. P–KR4. With those moves White keeps Black from breaking out of his confinement since . . . N–N5 and . . . B–N4ch (followed by . . . N–K2) are stopped. Those pawn moves would permit White to turn his attention to a real target, such as KR7; e.g., 1. P–QR3 R–R2 2. P–KR4 Q–B2 3. B–Q3! and 4. Q–K4.

1. . . .	R–R2
2. B–B5?!	B–N4ch!
3. K–N1	N–K2

Black turned the momentum around with this gain of time. His bishops eventually decided the game White relied on another pretty but faulty move: 4. Q–K4 NxB 5. QxN P–Q4! 6. Q–Q3 P–Q5 7. Q–K4? (this should be the knight's square) R–K1 8. P–KR4 B–K2 9. Q–B4 B–K3 10. N–K4 P–QR4! 11. N–N3 Q–Q4 12. P–N3 P–R5 13. P–B4 Q–Q1! 14. N–R5 PxP 15. PxP Q–R1 16. N–Q2 R–Q1 17. K–B1 R–R8ch 18. N–N1 Q–R7 19. Q–K4 P–Q6 and after 20. N–B6ch BxN White resigned.

Getting Fancy

When you have a choice between two equally effective moves, one routine, the other pretty, most players become Paul Morphy.

We play chess to win but winning isn't enough. We like to think we can also create positions of beauty.

The flaw in this is partly psychological. If there really are two *equally effective* methods of gaining the advantage, your choice is open. But too often a player will be swayed by the urge to "Morphyize" a position. In an effort to play brilliant chess like the great nineteenth-century champion, they blind themselves without knowing it.

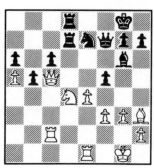

Sämisch–Vidmar, Karlsbad 1929
White to move

| 1. PxP! | RxN |
| 2. PxB | QxP(3) |

White's little combination completes a skillfully played middlegame. Black could not permit 3. B–K6 and so had to allow White to take a decisive material edge with 3. RxN R–Q8ch 4. B–B1.

But White wants to crown his success with an even prettier winning idea. It seems even more effective—as well as being more attractive—than 3. RxN because Black doesn't even get a check.

3. QxN??!	QxR
4. B–K6ch	K–R1
5. B–Q5!	

This remarkable move, similar to that of a famous game by Richard Reti, seems to win immediately. Black cannot protect his

first rank and his rook at the same time. After 5. . . . R–KN1 6.
BxR KxB 7. Q–K8 it is mate anyway.

5. . . .   **P–R4??**

Both players are so impressed with White's combination that
they overlook 5. . . . R–KN1! 6. BxR R–Q7! 7. Q–R4 (else mate on
the second rank) 7. . . . Q–B4ch and 8. . . . KxB, which gives
Black winning chances to think about.

       6. QxRch   **K–R2**
       7. B–K4ch??

Another hangover effect of White's "brilliant" combination.
He is so carried away by his success that he commits a final
blunder. With a check on KN8 it would have been all over.

7. . . .   **QxB!**

This desperadolike shot actually tips the advantage to Black
after 8. RxQ RxQ 9. R–K6 R–Q8ch 10. K–N2 R–QR8. But the
two players weren't ready for any more blunders—or brilliance
—and they drew here.

Sloppy errors can be committed in the name of art, as in this
example. Or they can be attributed to a different muse, that of
efficiency. But an overfinesse is an overfinesse.

Levenfish–Chekhover, Moscow 1935
White to move

After a spirited middlegame White is on the verge of liquidating into a won endgame. He can exchange pieces on KN7 now or wait a move, he thinks. Given that he puts off the liquidation for a move, you might assume he wasn't sure whether the king-and-pawn ending after 1. RxNch RxR 2. QxRch QxQ 3. BxQ KxB was a win. But in truth White had calculated as far as 4. K–N3 K–B3 5. K–B4 P–K4ch 6. K–K4 K–K3 7. P–R5! KxP 8. K–B5, after which White wins.

What happened was curious but not unusual. White may have calculated the winning liquidation but wasn't entirely certain his calculation was correct. So he took a tempo to make sure that it was a dead won ending.

1. P–N4??

Now after 2. RxNch and the wholesale liquidation, White's endgame task will be easier than the line already cited since he will be able to protect his QP with P–QB5.

1. . . .   **P–K4!**

White completely overlooked this trick. He cannot protect his vital pawns at KR4 and KB2 (2. QxKP QxP mates; 2. Q–N4 RxPch 3. R–N2 RxRch 4. KxR Q–Q7ch) any more. After 2. RxNch QxR he played on a few moves and then resigned. "Those whom the gods wish to destroy, they make mad," he said later.

Lasker's Law

Playing a good move is such an enjoyable experience that few players have the will power to restrain themselves. Enter any chess club or visit an open-air chess center at a park, and you will see players quickly—and usually loudly—making their choices known. But the best lesson to be learned about choosing a good move is how to sit on your hands.

When you see a good move, said Emanuel Lasker, *don't* play it. look for a better move. This advice from the great world champion is more important than anything you are likely to glean from an openings manual or endgame text.

Miagmasuren–Martens, Leningrad 1960—*1. P–K4 P–QB4 2. N–KB3 P–K3 3. P–Q4 PxP 4. NxP N–KB3 5. N–QB3 P–Q3 6. B–N5 B–K2 7. Q–B3 QN–Q2 8. 0–0–0 P–QR3 9. K–N1 Q–B2 10. Q–N3 N–N3?! 11. P–B4 P–R3 12. BxN BxB 13. N(4)–N5!? PxN 14. NxP Q–N1 15. P–K5! PxP 16. N–Q6ch K–B1 17. PxP Q–R2 18. P–QR3 B–K2 19. B–K2 N–Q4 20. KR–B1 BxN*

Position after 20. . . . BxN

21. RxPch!?

Temporarily two pieces down White suddenly sacrifices a rook. This decision shouldn't have been too great a surprise. White's pieces are all trained toward the Black king after 20. KR–B1. He sees that 21. PxB, the natural move, permits Black to consolidate with 21. . . . N–B3 (since 22. RxN PxR 23. P–Q7 can be handled by 23. . . . BxP 24. RxB R–R2 or 24. Q–Q6ch K–N2 25. Q–N3ch K–R2).

Therefore, White knows that his attack must begin showing results quickly and that the natural moves won't work. He looks for a sacrifice, and this kind of thinking is correct. His error is not looking long enough.

With 21. RxN! it's quickly apparent that White's attack is overwhelming. For example, 21. . . . PxR 22. Q–N6 P–QN4 23. B–R5! wins outright (23. . . . B–K3 24. QxB). The variations are so relatively easy to calculate and so clear-cut in their conclusions— unlike 21. RxPch—that White must have decided on the other sacrifice without considering 21. RxN.

21. . . .	KxR
22. B–R5ch	K–N1
23. R–KB1	

This promising, but unclear, position is what White foresaw when he sacrificed the rook. He threatens 24. B–B7ch K–B1 25. BxPch, which pulls the Black king to the center for a quick mate.

Black concluded that his position was critical since 23. . . . N–B3 24. RxN and 23. . . . BxP 24. QxB only encourage the attack and 23. . . . P–QN4 permits 24. Q–N6! threatening 25. R–B7 (24. . . . B–B1 25. RxBch KxR 26. Q–K8 mate; 24. . . . N–K2 25. R–B8ch!; 24. . . . Q–K2 25. PxB Q–N4 26. R–B8ch, etc.). What he didn't look for was the possibility of bringing his queen to the defense of the kingside with 23. . . . P–KN4! 24. Q–Q3 P–N4.

| 23. . . . | N–B6ch? |

If you've decided that you're lost, it doesn't hurt to set a few traps (24. PxN QxP, and White doesn't have enough checks to stop his own king from being mated). On 24. K–B1? N–K7ch or 24. K–R1 BxRP Black gets the last laugh.

| 24. QxN | R–R2 |
| 25. Q–B3? | |

The right order of moves is 25. PxB B–Q2 26. B–N6!, after which White's threats of 27. R–B7 and 27. Q–B3 are too much. For example, 26. . . . B–K1 27. P–Q7! BxB 28. Q–B8ch or 26. . . . B–N4 27. P–Q7 BxP 28. Q–B3 B–B3 29. Q–B7ch K–R1 30. Q–B8ch.

| 25. . . . | P–KN4? |
| 26. PxB | B–Q2 |

Notice that if Black had played 25. . . . P–KN3! 26. PxB B–Q2 White would have nothing more than a draw now since 27. BxP would be met by 27. . . . R–N2 (28. B–B7ch K–R1 29. Q–R3 K–R2).

27. B–B7ch	K–R1
28. Q–B6ch	R–N2
29. QxPch	R–R2

30. Q–B6ch	R–N2
31. P–KR4!	Q–R5
32. R–R1	**Resigns**

Black finally conceded because 32. . . . P–N5, while it keeps the deadly file closed for a few moves, permits 33. P–R5! and 34. P–R6.

Now let's recap.

(*a*) White was thinking well when he looked for a combination back at the diagram. His mistake was playing the first good-looking sacrifice he saw. 21. RxN would have won outright.

(*b*) Black made the reverse error. He became discouraged after 23. R–KB1 and played the desperate 23. . . . N–B6ch. His mistake was partly a failure to see the defense 23. . . . P–KN4. But we can also say that he failed to find the correct defense because he didn't look hard enough for it. He thought he was going to lose . . . and he lost.

(*c*) White made what we might call a sequence error at move 25. But it was more than a calculation slip. He erred because he saw how strong 25. Q–B3 was and stopped short of seeing how much stronger 25. PxB! was.

(*d*) Black finally put the game out of reach with an automatic 25. . . . P–KN4, gaining an escape square for the king. Of course, if Black knew that 25. . . . P–KN4 provided air for the king, he knew that 25. . . . P–KN3 did too. But Black didn't look to see whether there was a difference or whether the difference mattered. Both sides erred, but it is the final mistake that always counts.

Missed Opportunity

Why do we play second-best moves? Sometimes it's because we wouldn't know what the right move was if it stared us in the face. We simply don't consider *that* move, the correct move, to be favorable in our system of values.

But most of the time we must blame ourselves for simply not looking for the best move. Seek and ye shall find is as true on the chessboard as elsewhere.

"Why don't we look?" is another good question. Lasker's law offers one explanation: we stop looking once we've found a good move. The pitfall is especially dangerous when we're pursuing a strategic plan that is bearing fruit.

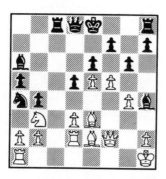

Pachman–Foltys, Prague 1946
White to move

1. Q–B4

White has achieved his thematic breakthrough at KB5. He can already visualize a winning finish. Once White brings a rook to KB1, Black will castle, and get mated after Q–R6 followed by P–B6 or R–B3–R3.

1. . . .   **NPxP?**
2. NPxP?!

The move played was adequate and enticed Black into a desperate counterattack (*2. . . . P–Q5?! 3. NxP B–N2ch 4. B–B3 BxBch 5. NxB Q–Q4 6. R–N2 B–K2 7. R–KB1 QxQP? 8. N–Q4 Q–R3 9. PxP PxP 10. Q–B7ch K–Q2 11. R–Q1 QR–K1 12. R–QB2 N–B6 and Black resigned*).

But wouldn't it have been even easier had White played 2. P–N5? That move might not have been thematic, but it would have won a clear piece. Yet White never looked for it.

An overriding attitude can have this blinding effect on a player who might otherwise be tempted to keep looking. He stops because he's found the move that approaches his strategic goal, adds to his tactical chances, or secures a solid position. He doesn't expect to find more no matter how long he looks.

This is amply demonstrated by the following position from a Soviet junior event.

Alburt–Georgadze, Vilna 1971
Black to move

Black, with the aid of a grandmaster trainer, subjected the above position and the ones that led to it to intensive analysis while the game was adjourned overnight. The two men looked long and hard and finally found that after forcing this position, they could save the game with this sequence:

| 1. ... | Q–N8 |

Now on 2. Q–K2 Q–R7 Black keeps the White king in a web of perpetual threats and checks (3. Q–K3 QxP or 3. Q–N4 Q–N8).

| 2. K–N4 | Q–K8 |
| 3. P–R4 | |

White had to do something about 3. . . . . N–B3 mate.

3. ...	N–B3ch
4. K–R3	Q–R8ch
5. K–N3	N–K5ch
6. K–N4	N–B3ch
7. K–N3	N–K5ch

Here the game was agreed drawn. Black was happy until someone pointed out 8. K–N4 Q–R7!, a move that wins immediately.

Black had calculated everything out with his grandmaster
aide. They had seen all the moves leading up to the final position.
What they didn't see was the correct evaluation of the position.
They were just looking for a draw.

Finally, we don't look for the best moves because we don't
realize the scope of our pieces. In the position after 23. R–KB1
on p. 188, Black didn't look for the right defense because it never
occurred to him that his queen, remote on QR2, could defend the
king on KN1. The queen didn't seem to have the capacity to affect
events on the other side of the world at KN2.

Malevinsky–Gefenas, Vilna 1978
Black to move

Here is a similar case of missed opportunity. Black would give
anything to avoid the exchange of queens. But he cannot afford
to let White play QxRch or B–Q6ch. For example, 1. . . . QxR
2. B–Q6ch K–R2 3. R–R1ch and 4. QxR leaves White with a
devastating attack.

1. . . .   QxQ??

After 2. RxQ White kept the attack and eventually won. The
remarkable feature is that, considering how much effort Black
must have spent to avoid the exchange of queens, he didn't find
the forced mate he can play in the diagram. If you can't, it's
because you aren't considering the range of the Black queen.

Yes, 1. . . . RxPch and 2. . . . Q–B7ch wins because the queen can come back to KR2.

Bad Moves in Bad Positions

In bad positions the margin of error shrinks. You can afford second-best moves in advantageous positions. Sometimes it takes half a dozen inferior moves to dissipate an advantage. But when you have an inferior game, one slight inaccuracy can be terminal.

The first task of the defender is to recognize that he stands worse and change his outlook. Only then can he appreciate the opportunities to cut his losses.

Petrosian–Spassky, Leningrad 1960
Black to move

In the preceding few moves Black had seized the initiative by advancing his queenside pawns. In return he granted White the powerful knight on QN5 and pawn on QB7. An almost imperceptible slip marred his risk-taking, and now Black should realize how much trouble he is in. His original plan of . . . P–KB4–5 made sense when White had a bishop on his KN3. Now the advance lacks punch.

1. . . .   **P–B4?**

An accurate evaluation of the position would reveal that White stood a bit better because of his passed QBP. This factor had less significance a few moves ago when Black's attack was brewing on the kingside. Now the attack is slow in getting started, and Black should consider cutting his queenside losses.

Two ways of cleaning up the queenside problem are *(1)* 1. . . . R–R3 followed by 2. . . . B–Q2 and 3. . . . BxN to win the BP (1. . . . B–Q2 immediately permits 2. NxQP QxN?? 3. B–R7ch) and *(2)* the direct 1. . . . QR–B1 and 2. . . . RxP. The first line kisses off any lingering hope of kingside attack since Black's white-square bishop is vital to that end. After 1. . . . R–R3 2. B–B2 B–Q2 3. N–Q2 for instance, Black's weakness on the white squares is apparent after 3. . . . BxN? 4. PxB R–N3 5. N–B4 or 3. . . . P–B4 4. P–N4!. But Black has good chances after 3. . . . P–Q4.

The exchange sacrifice 1. . . . QR–B1 2. B–B2 RxP!? is also promising since 3. NxR QxN gives Black excellent piece play. Black could return to kingside attack with . . . P–B4–5 knowing that his queenside was much more solid.

2. B–B2	P–B5

White didn't have to worry about 2. . . . P–K5 because of 3. Q–Q5ch and 4. KN–Q4. By pushing the other pawn Black concedes the K5 square to White.

3. PxP	NPxP
4. R–K1	R–R3

Black is a little late with this rook maneuver. He hasn't decided whether to liquidate the queenside situation yet and so stops to protect his QP.

5. B–K4	P–R4?

This was the last chance to do something about the queenside. With 5. . . . B–Q2 followed by 6. . . . BxN and 7. . . . R–N3 Black would be agreeing to play the lesser side of a middlegame with bishops of opposite colors. He is unwilling to lower his sights and presses on with the hope of attack. Notice that 5. . . . NxB 6. RxN B–B4 is a better way of pressing the attack, even though White is still better after 7. R–K2; e.g., 7. . . . P–K5 8. Q–Q5ch K–R1 9. KN–Q4.

6. Q–B2	Q–B3
7. N–Q2!	

White can defend solidly now that he controls the vital white squares. The game drew to a quick close: 7. . . . . P–KR5 8. P–B3 B–B1 9. B–Q5ch K–R1 10. N–K4 Q–R3 11. R–K2! P–R6 12. PxP R–B4 13. R–R2 P–R5 14. P–R4! P–N6 15. PxP PxP 16. Q–Q1 RxR 17. QxR *Black resigns*. Once the kingside attack was stilled, Black could not compete on the queenside.

The decision required is partly one of recognition—seeing the change of fortunes (p. 158)—and partly one of visualization. The latter consists of knowing what it takes to lose and what it takes to draw. The distinction between the two is very hard to pinpoint and mastery of it comes only through experience.

But we can identify some of the basic outlines of this distinction. For example, it is easier to lose a sharp, unbalanced but materially equal position than it is to lose a static, but pawn-down ending.

Hort–Portisch, Skopje, 1968—1. P–K4 P–K4 2. N–KB3 N–QB3 3. B–N5 P–QR3 4. BxN QPxB 5. 0–0 P–B3 6. P–Q4 PxP 7. NxP N–K2 8. N–QB3 N–N3 9. P–B4?! P–QB4 10. N–B3 QxQ 11. RxQ B–KN5 12. K–B2? B–Q3 13. N–Q5 0–0–0 14. P–B5 N–K4 15. B–B4 KR–K1 16. P–KR3 B–R4 17. R–K1 B–B2

Position after 17. . . . B–B2

White's premature advance of his KBP has given Black terrific piece play in the center. It is a long way from a win, but one can see the beginning of a substantial Black advantage already. To meet the threat of 18. . . . BxN 19. PxB NxN which would win a pawn, White could simplify with 18. NxN BxN(K) 19. BxB RxB.

But then Black's advantage is pronounced. The exchanges have only served to remove some of White's best defensive pieces and fatten the ratio of remaining well-developed pieces in Black's favor. For example, 20. P–B4 P–B3 or 20. N–B3 P–QN4 would put White in a big hole.

It is time to cut White's losses down to manageable proportions. White surely doesn't like to make such a decision. He would probably be surprised by the urgency of the matter, since it seems he hasn't made any grave errors so far. He certainly doesn't want to give up all chance of winning and play a boring defensive game for another thirty or forty moves.

Yet that is what is needed. With 18. QR–Q1! Black would have to cash in on his initiative immediately or lose all advantage. Play would then continue with 18. . . . NxN 19. KxN BxN 20. PxB (not 20. RxB BxB 21. RxRch RxR 22. KxB R–Q7!) 20. . . . BxB 21. KxB RxR 22. RxR RxP 23. R–K7. White would be a clear pawn behind, but his active rook and king promise good drawing chances.

18. N–B3?

This doesn't cost any material and prevents dangerous enemy incursions (18. . . . NxN 19. KxN BxB 20. KxB R–Q7 21. R–K2 and K–K3). It does make another concession, however, besides the obvious one of retreating a developed piece.

18. . . .	**N–Q6ch!**
19. PxN	**BxB**

White's loss in this game could be blamed on his surrender of the two bishops or on the weakening of his pawn structure—his QP is now a bad liability. But these are clinical explanations that ignore the true nature of White's collapse. It is comparable to saying a man died because his heart stopped pumping. That explanation says nothing about the causes of heart failure—his failure to restrict his diet, give up smoking, reduce stress, etc.

The final, terminal stages went like this: 20. QR–Q1 R–Q2 21. P–QN3 P–QN4 22. N–K2 B–Q3 23. K–K3 P–B5! 24. N–B1 (or 24. NPxP PxP 25. P–Q4 QR–K2 26. N–B3 B–N5) 24. . . . QR–K2 25. NPxP PxP 26. R–K2 B–Q4! 27. N–Q2 PxP 28. KxP B–B3 29. N(1)–N3 B–N4ch 30. N–B4 R–Q1! 31. N–Q2 B–N5ch 32. K–B2 KBxN White resigns in face of 33. R(2)xB B–R5ch.

Desperation and Surrender

The other extreme is premature surrender, or a last-ditch violent bid for salvation when the end is far from near. The causes of this malady are largely matters of attitude. You believe you're going to lose. You feel you deserve to lose because of your previous play. So . . . you lose.

In practical terms, we would say this is another misunderstanding of the distinction between losing and drawing. You can have an absolutely horrible position, lifeless and shot full of weaknesses. But if there is no way of exploiting those targets, there is no way of losing (aside from rare occasions such as zugzwang). In other words, you should never resign—or become desperate—unless absolutely certain of your opponent's winning *plan.*

Tal–Matanovic, Bled 1961
Black to move

By all rights, Black should be dead lost. White has a substantial material edge in real terms—a queen and a strong passed KRP against rook, knight, and two pawns. The game should end very quickly and it did.

1. . . .	N–B3??
2. BxR	NxBch
3. K–K1	N–B3
4. Q–R8	P–R4 and resigns

Black had gone through with the formality of sealing his last move and resigning the following day rather than continue the adjourned game. However, he could have made it a very lively adjournment had he played 1. . . , R–N5!. White would have had to sacrifice his queen (2. Q–R8 R–N7ch 3. B–K2 N–B3 followed by 4. . . . B–N5 or 4. . . . R–N1) with 2. BxB RxQ 3. PxR in order to win.

Black assumed that such a position would have been just as hopeless as the one he resigned in. Black must lose his knight for a pawn after 3. . . . N–B3 4. B–R7! (4. . . . NxB 5. P–N8=Q) and play the rest of the game a piece behind. Yet the game is not at all clear. After 3. . . . N–B3 4. B–R7 N–N1 (the most accurate since it gives Black's king time to roam) 5. BxN K–B3 6. B–R7 KxP 7. B–B5 K–B3 8. B–B8 P–N3, White's winning plan is obscure. Black can keep the White king from advancing and play . . . P–R3 and . . . P–N4 at an appropriate moment.

But White never needed to work for the win. Black's premature surrender with 1. . . . N–B3, made the task academic.

This kind of fatalism can occur at any point in the game, not just the late ending. For example, in Milner–Barry vs. Alexander, London 1939, play went *1. P–K4 P–K4 2. N–QB3 N–QB3 3. B–B4 B–B4 4. Q–N4 K–B1 5. Q–N3 P–Q3 6. P–Q3 N–Q5 7. B–N3 B–K3 8. B–N5 Q–Q2 9. K–Q2 P–KR3 10. B–K3 N–KB3 11. KN–K2?? NxBch and White suddenly resigned (!)*. The decision was justified in part by Black's forced win of the queen with 12. . . . N–R4!. White can only obtain two minor pieces in compensation, so he resigned before the hammer fell.

But actually White can obtain a solid, although inferior, position after 12. RPxN N–R4 13. Q–R4 P–KN4 14. QxN B–N5 15. QxB! QxQ 16. BxB and 17. N–N3. With a strong knight on KB5 White can make it exceptionally difficult for Black to break through.

Errors with Material

Materialism is no mistake in chess. The game is essentially balanced from the first move: you start with the same number of pieces as your opponent and you never get to move twice in a row. Without some unbalancing, the game will end in a draw. Therefore, giving or taking material is the most radical effort to alter the balance. Sacrifices or material gains are rarely neutral moves—they are either good or bad. Here are the major material mistakes.

Greed

Not all material grabbing is greed, of course. In most games at all levels of skill it is the player who is ahead materially after thirty moves who eventually wins. Greed is "extreme or voracious desire," that is, wanting more than you need or deserve.

Kan–Botvinnik, Moscow 1935—1. P–K4 P–K4 2. N–QB3 N–KB3 3. P–B4 P–Q4 4. BPxP NxP 5. N–B3 N–QB3 6. Q–K2 B–KB4 7. Q–N5?! N–B4 8. P–Q4 P–QR3 9. Q–K2 N–K5 10. Q–K3 NxN 11. PxN BxP! 12. Q–B2 B–KB4 13. N–R4 B–K3 14. B–Q3 Q–Q2 15. 0–0 N–R4 16. N–B5 0–0–0! 17. Q–K2 Q–B3 18. R–N1 P–R3 19. B–Q2 N–B5 20. N–K3

Position after 20. N–K3

Black correctly grabbed a queenside pawn at move 11 and took steps to hold the pawn with a concentration of pieces on that side of the board. His well-placed knight blocked White's best attacking diagonal (K2–QR6) and neutralized dangers along the QN-file (21. R–N3 and 22. KR–N1 would be met by 22. . . . N–R4). White realized this and sought to rid the board of the defender, but 20. . . . B–K2 or 20. . . . K–N1 would give Black excellent winning chances. For example, 20. . . . B–K2 21. NxN PxN 22. B–K4 B–Q4 23. BxB QxB 24. Q–N4ch K–N1 25. QxP?? KR–N1 with a skewer along the KN-file.

20. . . .	**NxN?**
21. BxN!	

Perhaps Black counted on 21. QxN B–K2 with a useful gain of time (. . . B–N4) coming up. He misread the position, thinking that White couldn't give away another pawn. It was still time for 21. . . . B–K2.

21. . . .	**QxP??**

There is no real reason for this. Of all the pawns to win, this is the most dangerous because it opens up another attacking file and gives White too many tempos to continue the assault. The extra pawn, it's true, will increase Black's chances in the ending. But one pawn is enough to play for a win.

22. KR–B1	**Q–R4**
23. Q–B2	**P–QB3**

24. B–Q2	Q–B2
25. Q–R4	

There is no longer any defense. White threatens both 26. B–R5 and 26. BxQRP. Compare White's domination of the queenside with the previous diagram. Botvinnik played 25. . . . R–Q2 and resigned after *26. BxQRP.*

Negative Sacrifice

A sacrifice can be an offer of material to acquire a tangible positional asset (i.e., weakening the enemy pawns, getting the better minor pieces, etc.). But in this case we mean the reverse: sacrificing the positional soundness of your game to win material. Often this means grabbing a pawn unwisely. It is not greed per se, since greed is usually a lust for material when you don't need any more than you already have. This error is rather a matter of strategic desperation, as in the following:

Dely–Simagin, Moscow 1962—*1. P–K4 P–QB4 2. N–KB3 P–Q3 3. P–Q4 PxP 4. NxP N–KB3 5. N–QB3 P–QR3 6. B–QB4 P–K3 7. B–N3 B–K2 8. P–B4 0–0 9. P–B5 P–K4?! 10. N(4)–K2 QN–Q2 11. N–N3 P–QN4 12. B–N5 B–N2 13. BxN NxN 14. N–R5! NxN 15. QxN R–B1 16. B–Q5*

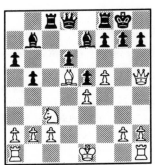

Position after 16. B–Q5

White has deftly obtained a strategic edge through his conquest of the Q5 square. Once the white-square bishops are exchanged, he will be able to post a knight on that key observation point, whereas Black's remaining bishop will look anemic on the black squares.

Black should realize that strong measures are required. For example, 16. . . . P–N5!?. After 17. N–K2 BxB 18. PxB Black doesn't need to fear the Q4 outpost any longer and can safely play 18. . . . RxP. The critical line is 17. BxB PxN 18. BxR PxP 19. R–Q1 Q–R4ch, after which Black obtains good play for a minimal amount of material sacrificed.

16. . . .	BxB?

But this kind of negative positional sacrifice leaves White in command of the board within a few moves.

17. NxB!	RxP
18. 0–0	B–N4

Aside from 19. P–B6 White also threatens 19. QR–B1! with a huge bind. Black's pieces would quickly run out of moves. As played, Black keeps his pieces alive—but not his king.

19. P–B6 P–R3 (19. . . . BxP 20. RxB! PxR 21. R–KB1 wins quickly) 20. R–B5! (threatens 21. RxB PxR 22. N–K7ch) R–B8ch 21. RxR BxR 22. Q–Q1! BxP 23. Q–Q2 B–Q5ch 24. K–R1 R–K1 (24. . . . K–R2 25. R–R5 R–R1 26. Q–N5 R–N1 27. N–K7!) 25. R–N5! P–N3 26. R–R5! Black resigns.

Holding Onto Material That Can't Be Held

A realistic attitude toward the material balance is vital. If it's clear that you are going to lose something or that trying to hold the balance will compromise your game irrevocably, you must start looking around for a way to get compensation.

Chess is a constant shift of varying strengths and weaknesses. So when one of your weaknesses is doomed to exploitation, it's time to pay attention to your strengths.

Geller–Jansa, Budapest 1970
Black to move

It's no secret that Black's QP is in great danger. It can't be protected again on Q5, and it is unlikely that it will be any stronger on Q6. A true appreciation of this would lead Black to search for counterplay. Had he done so he would probably have found 1. . . . Q–N4! 2. P–N3 Q–B3!. That maneuver threatens to protect the QP with 3. . . . R–Q1 but also to mate with 3. . . . Q–B6. After 3. NxP R–Q1 4. Q–B3 Black can simply sit on the position with 4. . . . P–N3 and 5. . . . B–N2, having two excellent bishops to make up for his pawn.

What he did, however, was focus on the QP and make oversights that ended the game quickly.

1. . . .	P–Q6?
2. Q–K3!	R–B1?
3. RxP	Q–B3
4. R–Q7! and wins.	

Forcing the Mechanical Sacrifice

Most successful sacrifices stem from poor previous play by the defending player. By the time a sacrifice is offered the defender has already made the mistakes that will doom him. When Adolf Anderssen, the nineteenth-century world champion, crowned his games with sacrifices, it was only after outplaying his opponents in the early struggle. But when his fans asked why he hadn't been able to sacrifice brilliantly against Paul Morphy, Anderssen explained: "Morphy wouldn't let me."

Probably the most common error involving sacrifices is the permission—often the encouragement—of a standard or mechanical sacrifice. It may be called mechanical because it is so frequently seen and so easily followed up that it can be considered a routine matter.

Nikitin–Kanko, Leningrad 1957
Black to move

Here is a typical sacrifice-prone position in that most tactical of openings, the Sicilian Defense. In this and many similar positions White can consider sacrifices such as NxKP, BxNP, N–B5, or N–Q5. In the first two cases White will gain two pawns for a piece and keep the enemy king in the center for a while. In the latter two, White may only get one pawn, but he will also open up a key file (e.g., N–Q5/ . . . PxN/KPxP) and obtain vital squares for his assault army. Of the four likely sacrifices, N–Q5 is White's soundest in the position above.

But the move is Black's. He can anticipate most of the sacrificial possibilities with 1. . . . 0–0. But that would be another case of "castling into it" (2. P–K5 PxP 3. BxN NxB 4. P–K5 threatening PxN and QxRP mate). 1. . . . 0–0–0 is better, although this invites BxNP at some future point. But that is certainly preferable to:

1. . . .   P–N5?
2. N–Q5!

Black not only ignored this dangerous "sac," he virtually forced it. White, if he had any doubts about the soundness of his offer, would have been persuaded by considering the alternative, 2. N(4)–K2 R–QB1, which gives Black an excellent game and stops virtually all of White's attacking plans. Now Black has little choice since 2. . . . NxN 3. PxN BxB 4. PxB gives White an equally good attack for only a pawn.

2. . . .	**PxN**
3. PxP	**K–B1**

The threats were 4. N–B5 and 4. RxBch (e.g., 3. . . . K–Q1 4. RxB KxR 5. N–B5ch K–B1 6. NxNP! KxN 7. B–R6ch or 5. . . . K–Q1 6. NxNP followed by N–R5). Now White can play 4. RxB just as well, but his preference is also good.

4. N–B5	**B–Q1**
5. B–R6!	

This destroys all defense since 5. . . . PxB 6. QxPch is a quick mate. White ended the game by getting all his material back with interest.

5 . . . R–KN1 6. BxPch RxB 7. Q–R6 N–R4 8. P–N4! B–KB3 9. PxN Q–R4 10. NxR BxN 11. QxQPch K–N1 12. R–N1 QxRP 13. RxBch KxR 14. R–N1ch K–R1 15. Q–R6 Black resigns.

Failing to Sacrifice When Necessary

There are times when a "sac" is not only desirable but vital. Here it is not a question of giving up something that will be lost inevitably. It is rather a question of parting with material because of the danger of being swamped positionally or of being mated if the enemy is left alone. The sacrifice, often a countersacrifice to a previous offer by the opponent, is necessary to gain time to beat off the opponent's attack.

Geller–Kotov, Moscow 1952
Black to move

White has a vigorous initiative brewing but has given up a pawn and exchanged a bishop for a knight. This latter factor creates the possibility of a countersacrifice to beat off the impending Q–R5 and N–B5.

1. . . .	R–K2?

True, this defends KB2 against 2. Q–R5 and saves the attacked rook as well, but a deeper look into the position would have convinced Black of the seriousness of his plight. He could have squelched all immediate attacking threats against him with 1. . . . RxN! 2. RxR NxP and retained good winning chances with two pawns for the exchange.

2. Q–R5	P–R3
3. N–B5!	RxRch
4. RxR	PxN
5. R–K3	

This is the followup Black underestimated or overlooked when he played 1. . . . R–K2 and 2. . . . P–R3. If Black permits 6. R–R3 it is all over. And on 5. . . . P–N5 White has a neat finish with 6. N–R6ch PxN 7. QxNPch K–R2 8. Q–B5ch K–N1 9. R–N3ch. Finally, 5. . . . P–B3, creating a flight square at KB2, is punished by 6. Q–N6!.

The game ended abruptly anyway.

5. . . .	B–B1
6. BxP!	BxB
7. R–K8ch	Resigns

The Panic Sacrifice

The reverse of Failing to Sacrifice When Necessary is the spasmodic "sac" of the player who overreacts to threats by going in for a desperate attacking try. Instead of defense, he is suddenly in control of the game, surprising his opponent with the initiative. But usually it fails.

Why? Well, as we indicated before, a sound sacrifice usually means that your position is strong enough to permit one. If you are in fact worse, it stands to reason that you can't afford to part with material. Such desperation sacs are playable only as a practical response to a certain loss.

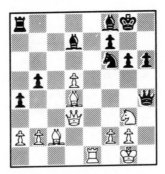

Tshcherbakov–Furman, Moscow 1952
White to move

White has been outplayed consistently since the opening and should worry about defense. Specifically, he must do something about 1. . . . N–N5. Rather than the solid but uninspiring 1. B–Q1, he heads for adventure.

1. R–K6?!

Now on 1. . . . N–N5 White has 2. RxPch! winning.

1. . . .	**PxR**
2. QxPch	**B–N2**
3. N–K4	**R–KB1**

Black easily covers the threatened 4. NxNch which would be met by 4. . . . RxN 5. BxR QxB keeping an extra piece. White can now try to open more lines with 4. PxP, but after 4. . . . BxP 5. NxNch RxN 6. Q–K8ch Black defends easily with 6. . . . B–B1. There is one other try, but Black's extra material and natural positional edge permit him to refute it with elegance:

4. P–N3	**QxN!**

And White resigned shortly after noticing that his queen would be trapped with 5. . . . B–K1.

Misunderstanding What Constitutes Compensation

When you give up material you must expect something solid in return—other material, dangerous threats, positional strengths, or some combination of these. Even if you regain a theoretical equality of material, an imbalance may still remain on the board. For instance, two pawns and a knight obtained as compensation for your sacrificed rook may be no match for the rook in the next stage of the game. Theoretically, it's enough. Practically, it isn't.

Compensation is a very hard quantity to evaluate because you must be able to judge the activity of pieces in the near future. When the fireworks ignited by your sacrifice have subsided, who will hold the initiative and for how long?

Westerinen–Ivkov, Geneva 1977—*1. P–Q3 P–KN3 2. N–KB3 B–N2 3. P–KN3 P–QB4 4. B–N2 N–QB3 5. 0–0 P–K4 6. N–B3 KN–K2 7. P–K4 P–Q3 8. N–KR4 0–0 9. P–B4 PxP 10. BxP B–K3 11. Q–Q2 P–Q4 12. B–R6 P–Q5 13. N–Q5 P–B3 14. BxB KxB*

Position after 14. . . . KxB

White's opening gave him a promising game from both a positional and attacking point of view. His pawn offer was quite sound (13. . . . NxN 14. PxN BxP 15. KBxB QxB 16. N–B5! PxN 17. BxB KxB 18. Q–N5ch K–R1 19. Q–B6ch K–N1 20. RxP and 21. R–N5ch). But now he has to choose between trying to mate or trying to win positionally. Exchanging his black-square bishop was a poor move positionally although it increased his short-range attacking chances. Still, 15. N–B4 followed by N–B3 and R–B2 is the best plan.

15. NxBP??

This is all wrong. White will get the technical compensation of three pawns, all passed, for the knight. And for a few moves the Black king will be kicked around and forced to seek refuge on the queenside.

But what is crucial in evaluating such a sac is the position four or five moves from now. After White gets his pawns he will be left with a queen, a bad bishop, and a rook to compete against Black's coordinated force. The pawns will be able to advance only in an ending—and only then with great care. The late middlegame belongs entirely to Black's knight.

15. . . .	RxN
16. RxR	RxR
17. Q–R6	K–B2!

This is the only critical move for Black in the game. The king heads off to safety at Q2 after which Black will enjoy the initiative until White's resignation. The remainder went *18. QxRPch K–K1 19. NxP NxN 20. QxNch K–Q2 21. P–B3 Q–R1!* (This is the position White misjudged. Black's threats of . . . PxP and . . . R–KN1 are too much.) *22. Q–N5 PxP! 23. QxP PxP 24. R–N1 P–N3 25. Q–R3 Q–Q5ch 26. K–R1 N–N5 27. Q–R4ch K–K2 28. Q–R3 R–QB1 29. P–R3 P–R4 30. QxNP QxQ 31. RxQ R–B7 32. R–N1 BxQRP 33. R–Q1 B–N6 White resigns.*

Overlooking the Countersacrifice

When you give up material there is a tendency to lose track of how much. If the final reward of your sacrifice is a mating attack, it won't matter how much. But if your attack can be broken by a countersacrifice—a return of material by the enemy—the question becomes, How much is too much?

Lilienthal–Nezhmetdinov, Moscow 1954
White to move

This is an exceptionally difficult position to evaluate. White "has the attack" in the sense that Black's king is subject to more immediate harassment from enemy pieces than White's king. But Black has sacrificed a pawn to obtain excellent positional compensation—chiefly in the form of his center pawns and active bishops.

The temporary initiative enjoyed by White should be used carefully, such as with 1. R–K1 and 2. B–B3—moves aimed at consolidating and neutralizing a potentially explosive position.

1. BxP?!

You can't fault White for cleverness. With this sacrifice he turns his kingside pieces into attackers: 1. . . . NxB (1. . . . BxN 2. RxB) 2. N–R5ch K–B2 3. R–B3ch regaining the piece at a profit.

1. . . .	NxB
2. N–R5ch	K–R3
3. R–R3	

White had examined the position this far when he calculated 1. BxP. His rook will deliver a murderous discovered check if Black doesn't have a good reply. In calculating this far, White couldn't consider every possible reply by his opponent—there are simply too many of them. But by focusing on the possible refutations of the sacrifice, he can be reasonably certain that he has sacrificed well.

Here the chief attempts at refutation are 3. . . . K–N4 and 3. . . . QxR, the two moves that take the sting out of White's threatened discovered check. White probably dismissed the king move after seeing that he could bring his queen into action after 3. . . . K–N4 4. Q–Q2ch K–B4 (4. . . . B–B5 5. NxB NxN 6. P–KN3) 5. Q–Q3ch. And he may have dismissed the queen sacrifice on the grounds that Black got insufficient material.

3. . . .	QxR!
4. PxQ	KxN

But Black has more than ample compensation if you remember the original piece he captured (1. . . . NxB). Now, with *two* minor pieces and a rook facing a disrupted White kingside, it turns out that the White king is the most vulnerable. A queen counter-sacrifice ended the game abruptly.

5. QxP	R–B6!
6. N–Q4	RxKRP
7. N–K2	N–B5
8. NxN	BxN
9. K–N2	R–QB1!

White resigned since Black will mate with 10. . . . R–N1ch 11. KxR B–B1 once the White queen leaves QB5.